We Choose Joy

How 22 Women went Beyond Healing to Create Joyful Lives

Curated by

Linda Laird Staszewski

Aurora Corialis Publishing

Pittsburgh, PA

WE CHOOSE JOY: HOW 22 WOMEN WENT BEYOND HEALING TO CREATE JOYFUL LIVES

For more information, address cori@auroracorialispublishing.com

Paperback ISBN: 978-1-958481-13-4

Ebook ISBN: 978-1-958481-14-1

Library of Congress Control Number: 2023916432

Printed in the United States of America

Cover by Karen Captline, BetterBe Creative

Edited by Allison Hrip, Aurora Corialis Publishing

Praise for We Choose Joy

"In this book, you will be inspired by 22 women who share their profound story and journey through the trials and trauma that led to their truth, transformation, and triumphant healing that empowered them to go on to cultivate a life filled with JOY and of contribution and community. You will shed tears, but you will rejoice in the resilience of these women in a way that will touch your heart and may empower you to make a change or tell YOUR story, causing the impact of this book to continue."

~ Patty Farmer, CEO/Marketing & Media Strategist, International Speaker, Podcast Host, Magazine Publisher

---

"*We Choose Joy* offers the reader a combination of collaboration and insights on overcoming difficult times and continuing to seek, create, and *choose joy* each and every day. This anthology provides reflection, inspiration, and shared hope. It offers a roadmap for how *they* did it. Twenty-two women share their relatable challenges, their vulnerabilities and struggles to transcend on their quest to choose joy."

~Heidi Parr Kerner M.A., Bestselling Author of *Step Into Your Spotlight*, Motivational Speaker, Visibility Coach

---

"This book delivers equal measures of inspiration and heartbreak. Each chapter introduces us to a remarkable person. *We Choose Joy* puts me in mind of the joy of doing psychotherapy, meeting one after another courageous person. It also put me in mind of Hippocrates' dictum, 'Before you offer to help someone, ask them if they are willing to give up the thing that is making them sick.' These twenty-two women bring honesty, courage, and heart to the process of freeing themselves from past trauma and conflict. You will want to re-read this book and get to know them better, and perhaps see yourself in their journeys."

~ Peter von Korff, Ph.D., Clinical Psychologist

"This book is a moving testament to the power of the human spirit and individual will to conquer adversity and find happiness. This living tribute honors the strength of these women to overcome grief and trauma by looking it in the face, refusing to remain victims, acknowledging their losses and pain, and planning for their brighter futures. This anthology will leave you feeling hopeful and inspired to take control of your life, let God in it, and find lasting joy."

~ Dr. Mary M. Iwanenko, OTD, MS, OTR/L, Gannon University First Lady and Director of the University Health Center

---

"I loved reading the stories of these dynamic women, led by their personal perseverance, as they pursued a path of trust and faith in God. They were ultimately emboldened by the realization that through their dire experiences, they had reached a spiritual evolution of self-empowerment, and gratitude, divinely orchestrated!"

~ Gay S. Hilton, Doctor of Natural Medicine, Facilitator/Speaker, Author of *Good Vibes...Bad Vibes!*

"My takeaways from this incredible book begin with Linda's chapter. To know Linda is to experience joy. When you read this chapter, you may have to ask yourself how she does it—staying joyful in the eye of the adversity tornado. When you read her story, you will discover what is at the root of all her joy and passion.

"Reading this book touched me, especially how these women exude joy even after significant trauma.

"Tharifa and I have an unbreakable bond. We shared our stories and life experiences. She rose from the ashes more than once, as did I. Everywhere Tharifa went, she was helping, educating, and informing. Due to her health and wellness business, workouts, and healthy eating plans, she could have easily passed as 20 years younger than her 64 years. She would share those secrets and love of life with everyone. I will never recover from the loss of my soul sister, Tharifa.

"Cathi, who goes by 'GG' ('God Girl') with her friends, has always shown the joyful love of God to everyone. Cathi shares intimate, deep trauma in this chapter that may have crushed many other women. She found a way to save herself and dedicated her life to spreading and sharing love with others. Be immersed in the joy that shines from GG.

"I also found a spiritual connection with Rachelle Bryant and her story. To take in the entire trauma she endured and experience her true joy for life and her family makes you ponder. Despite her life struggles, she takes the time to educate and help others understand trauma bonds—a remarkable woman.

"Finally, I must mention dear sweet Houng's story. She brings you through her childhood trauma. You experience the sweetness of her soul as she dedicates her life to feeding malnourished children. No matter what life throws her way, Houng uses her belief in God to bring her through triumphantly—what a fantastic story of courage, determination, and complete reliance on the Lord.

"I highly recommend this book. It will bring you joy, and give you great perspective as you move forward in your own life."

~ Thasia Anne Lunger, BSW; Author of *Check Mates*, *Horse Sense*, *Sea Escapes*, and *How Far Must I Go?*

"*Riveting!* Each chapter chronicles an incredible awakening in the author. Their vulnerabilities kept me on the edge of my seat to the point of liberation and celebration in my soul. God's grace covered every traumatic experience in their pursuit of finding JOY. *We Choose Joy: How 22 Women Went Beyond Healing to Create Joyful Lives* is a literary masterpiece!"

~ Dr. Linda D. Lee, CEO of LL Media Group, LLC & Lee Coaching and Consulting; Doctorate of Religious Philosophy in Pastoral Psychology; Professional Certified Life Coach; Certified Christian Mentor; Certified Mental Health First-Aider

---

"The experiences shared in this book are incredible demonstrations of God's saving grace. Although the stories are sad and shocking at times, it's beautiful to see how God has given each woman strength to overcome and continue to become all that He has planned. We are stronger together, and these women are breaking down walls with the power of their testimonies!"

~ Lori Clapper, Program Director, WCTL Radio

"The authors of *We Choose Joy* share personal experiences to encourage us to keep pushing forward for greater things. I am inspired that the authors' stories are relatable to many different people from different generations and cultures. These women are stronger than ever and more determined to help us persevere despite our circumstances. I was in tears reading this book, as I thought about my life and how to move past the challenges that I have/will face to find JOY! This is an amazing collection that needs to be shared!"

~ Dr. Matasha Murrell Jones, D.Mgt, MBA, CPC, CDMP

"The book *We Choose Joy* is a collection of powerful stories from women who have lived through and overcome unimaginable hardship and trauma. In spite of these experiences the authors find the strength to rise above their pasts, striving for fulfillment in their lives and beyond that, joy.

"I was immediately drawn to the concept of this unique anthology of women's writings and appreciate its inspirational joy. I am reminded of a dear friend who experienced a tragic loss. She dealt with her grief through finding joy in everyday moments and bringing joy to others at every opportunity.

"Joy is a positive energy. This energy allows one to live in the present, calling on an inner power, which fuels the ability to take positive steps forward to a brighter tomorrow.

"Thank you to all the women who shared their personal journeys."

~ Lorraine Dolan, Wife, Mom, Voter, Lifelong Volunteer, Candidate for Political Office

---

"I tell my children and students that life is about the journey and the everyday decisions that we make. This book tells the story of women who chose to keep living and to find joy beyond the darkness. No matter what your roadblock may be, you will find a story to relate to here and the hope that inspires. You could see these women as victims of various tragedies, abuses or illness, until you realize that they have found strength from their experiences. They have walked their path and emerged as warriors who are making a difference in the world around them with a joy that surpasses all understanding."

~ Melissa D. Burns, 4-time US Unlimited Aerobatic Team Member, Embry-Riddle Aeronautical University Professor, Alaska Airlines Pilot, Mother, Athlete

———

"From the first page of *We Choose Joy*, each author was vulnerable, relatable, and utterly human. I found myself rooting for them, crying with them, and celebrating their triumphs like they were my friends. In the chapter, 'A Prayer for Rain,' Dr. Andrea Jeffress has an extraordinary gift to effortlessly transport readers into her story filled with emotion, inspiration, and transformation.

"It's a must-read! Their words stay with you long after you've turned the last page. Their journeys to joy have left an indelible mark on my heart, and I can't wait to see what other life-changing stories these women share next."

~ Desiree Lee, Speaker and CEO, Authors In Business

———

"What an amazing book! I particularly enjoyed Dr. Andrea's heartbreaking, courageous and inspiring, story. Her gut-wrenching childhood memories of life with a father who struggled with addiction and recovery is a story of pain, love, and finally redemption. She reminds us that, with faith and a deep belief, there is nothing too hard for God. As each author shares her own emotional and moving transformation, we are all inspired to choose joy in our own lives. *We Choose Joy* is a must read for anyone yearning for hope and a new beginning amidst the storms of life."

~ Kelechi A. Uduhiri, MD, MPH, MS, FAAFP; Family & Preventive Medicine; CEO/Founder, Envision Wellness, LLC; Fellow, American Academy of Family Physicians; Bestselling Author of *Just What the Doctor Ordered*

"I connected with so many of the stories from We Choose Joy, and I'm sure that other women will too. One that stood out to me was Taira Ruzzi's. It was not only emotional and inspiring but also brave! This story is one that many have endured and few are able to share. Taira shares her experience of sexual assault and her journey in overcoming this traumatic event. Through a roller coaster of emotions from confusion to low self-worth Taira tells her story in overcoming this experience and not letting it dictate her life. Taira shares her journey of self-reflection and the deep inner work she took to heal herself, believe in herself, and grow from this unfair and traumatizing event. And that she did! Heroic, brave, strong, and inspiring is what you will take from this beautiful story of resilience, self-love, and vulnerability. This story gives hope and shows healing can be done! Taira mentioned a quote from Dr. Levine in her story, 'Trauma is a fact of life. It does not have to be a life sentence.'"

~ Safia Kassir, Owner of On Trend Social Marketing

"Twenty-two resilient women healing with joy! These strong women at first felt fear, then had the ability to recognize 'what they feared'! They learned how to put all behind them, to understand why it happened! The past existed, but does not any longer!"

~ Peggy Schwab Area Leader, Park Lane Jewelry; Zumba Instructor, Fitness U; Coauthor of *20 Lives Ignited*

In Loving Memory of
Tharifa Noor

This book is dedicated to our dear friend and fellow author Tharifa, a strong, ultra-positive, and amazing woman, who, through her legacy, will continue to touch so many lives with her stories of love, giving, courage and joy.

ALOHA, dear Tharifa ...

"She made broken look beautiful and strong look invincible. She walked with the universe on her shoulders and made it look like a pair of wings."

– Ariana Dancu

Her Light Still Shines

A Poem Honoring Tharifa Noor

By Cathi Gg Mitchell

Her light shone bright for the world to see.
She didn't dare hide it but rather she put it on a pedestal as a beacon.
A light in the darkness for lost souls to find their way.
A sturdy candle in the wind of life's storms.
A flame she shared to ignite the hearts of others with life, love, and passion.
No hesitation or fear that it would diminish her shine.
Which made it illuminate that much brighter.
You just needed to be in her vicinity to benefit from the warmth of her shine.
There were so many attempts to extinguish her light.
But it's impossible to completely put out a light like hers.
One that is meant to shine!
With every time that she gave of herself, the world was a little less dark.
Whether the impact she created on others was a lasting flame, a torch, a flicker, or a spark.
Each person she ignited continues to ignite others, and that continues on.
So, yes, while her personal light may have been snuffed out.
She will continue to illuminate the world with her beautiful brilliant light.
Because her light still shines.

Honeybee

By Cori Wamsley

Tharifa reminded me of a honeybee.
Small but energized.
Buzzing everywhere.
Nurturing. Making sure everyone had enough.
Uplifting. Loving. Caring.
She always had a word to heal, to help. Always had the time to share what was needed.
She had a big story. And big dreams.
She put her all into everything and everyone.
And suddenly, this beautiful soul is gone.
This is her chapter from 20 Lives Ignited, and another of her stories will be in We Choose Joy. Her impact lives on.

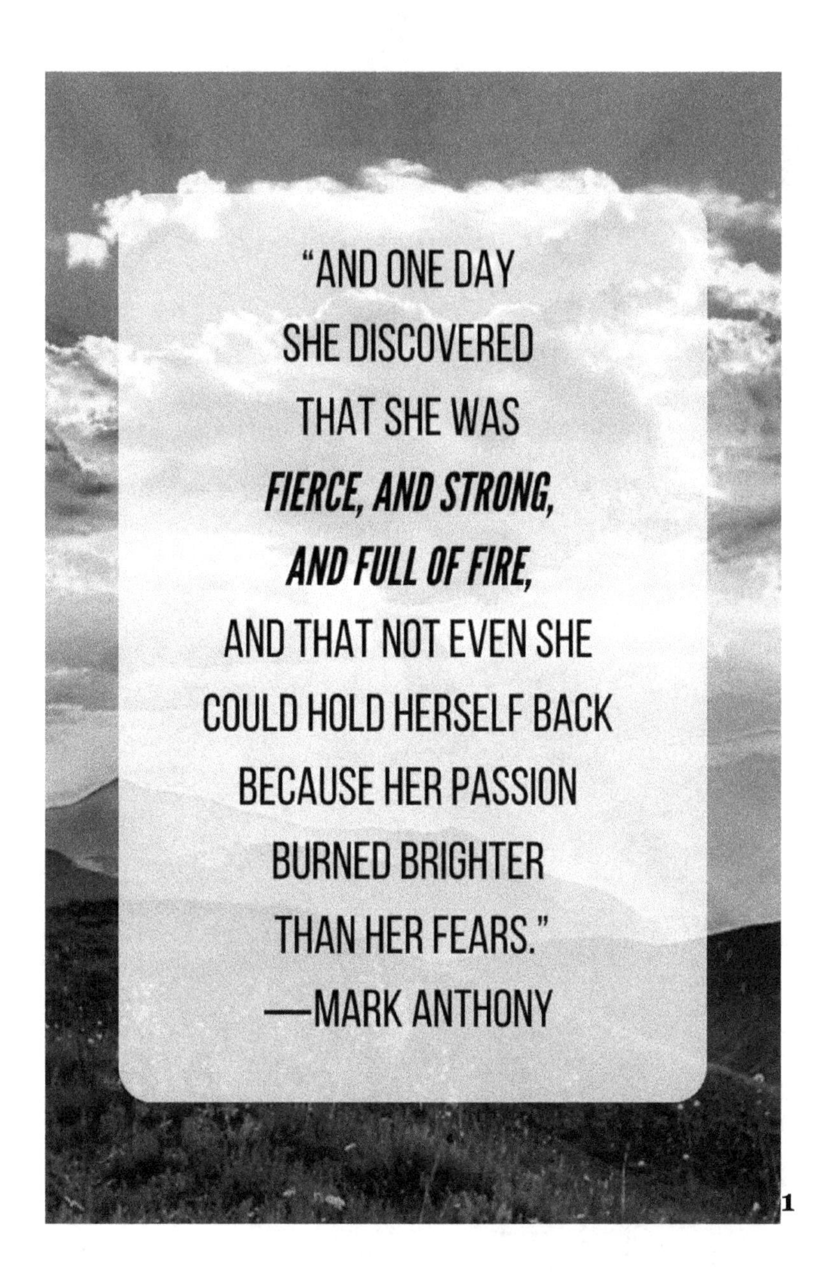

[1]

[1] Anthony, Mark. *The Beautiful Truth*. CreateSpace Independent Publishing Platform. 2016.

Table of Contents

Introduction

Linda Laird Staszewski

I am an aging advocate, creativity coach, and curator and author of two bestselling books.

I continually strive to inspire others to live their *best lives*. Ironically, I met my childhood goals of becoming an artist (sculpting and creating) and a teacher, with my workshops and mentoring, later in life. God is so good!

I married the love of my life, Tom, at the age of 25. We moved to Reading, Pa., where we lived for two years. We quit our jobs and moved to Pittsburgh, Pa., to be closer to our families, who both resided in our hometown of Erie, Pa. My beloved dad had been ill with cancer, and we wanted to be closer to home.

After working all day as an industrial engineer technician, I drove down to the city and attended night classes while living in Pittsburgh. It took me nine years to earn up through my master's degree in professional leadership/organizational development. It wasn't easy, and it was a huge sacrifice, but it was worth it. I was given this opportunity and did my best to grow with it. I have always believed in life-long-learning ... and I still do.

The company I was working for routinely paid for employees to attend school for job-related curriculums. This allowed me to move into the position of industrial engineer, then the plant engineer. Daily duties included time/method analysis, productivity, efficiency, working with engineering to build a detox room, and conveying the company's sewage treatment plant over to the township. Sometime later, I managed plant maintenance employees, who diligently kept the plant working with machinery, office air conditioning/heat, electrical issues, and so forth. Did I know mechanical engineering? No, but I told the team that although I did not have their talents and skills, working together, we could progress ... and we did! It was challenging, as back then, there weren't many women working in traditionally male positions. Many of the shop employees resented me, and it was painful, but I grew through the experiences. Although there were numerous obstacles, the Lord smoothed the path before me. My empathy and respect increased for women who work in typical men's positions and what they had to endure.

At one point in my life, I became unemployed and slowly recovered from the devastating job loss. I went through depression and anxiety. What would I do now? It seemed my life was over. I had lost my purpose. But soon, I heard, *Trust in the Lord!* It was time to reinvent myself, to *let go and let God.* I prayed, and I brainstormed. I trusted in God. Creativity played a major role, as I figured things out and created my own success.

Escape to Create Workshops was born, which included making vision boards to help attendees clarify, set action plans, visualize, focus on, and achieve goals. Then came DIY Crafts Kit subscriptions, followed by Queens Comfort Boxes, a personalized gift box service. I created the Facebook page, Unwavering Women 60+: Live Your Best Life, a place where women could connect, learn, and share. I understood the glass ceiling and the inequities that women were up against, and I wanted to offer support and connection. My goal was to let women know that they can still become who they want to be: *they are never too old and it is never too late!*

I had always wanted to write a book, but like so many others, I started, life got in the way, and it never materialized. When I learned of the anthology concept, I wanted *in!* I knew that was the answer! When I was unable to find one to contribute to, I turned to prayer. I felt the Lord tap me on the shoulder and say, *Why not you?* I remember feeling such fear and terror. *Ho*w could I do this? I had no idea how or where to even begin. Would other woman want to invest and share in my dream? I trusted the Lord.

I listened and committed to the book, as it was my passion. I was 71 years old at the time.

So, I set out on a journey to create the first anthology, *20 Lives Ignited: How 20 Women Over 60 are Creating Success on Their Own Terms*. This anthology includes 20 strong, amazing women who have overcome obstacles in their lives to become their own success stories. Our mission is to be an inspiration and to motivate girls, women of all ages, and especially women over the age of 60. We want everyone to know *you're never too old*, and *it is never too late*. We've only just begun at age 60!

At the age of 72, it was time for the second anthology. Several women contacted me, inquiring if I would be curating another book. They wanted in, and we easily got 22 women! This book encompasses how strong women refused to allow life's difficulties to pull them down or steal their JOY. Difficult times did *not* define them. They learned from their situations, transcended through the difficult times, grew stronger, and created their own JOY.

What do we mean by "joy"? What are the differences between happiness and joy? Happiness is an outward expression. Joy endures difficult times, struggles, and challenges, and connects with meaning, turning them into purpose. We pursue happiness, but we *choose* joy.

In April 2023, with five of the authors from *20 Lives Ignited* returning and 17 new women committed to this book, we have 22 strong, amazing women with stories to share and legacies to leave! Our mission with this book is to inspire women to make wise decisions, to empower themselves, to grow through difficult times, to not let anything stop them, and to *choose* JOY! Thus, *We Choose Joy: How 22 Women Went Beyond Healing to Create Joyful Lives* was born.

So, we encourage you to read these stories with an open heart and mind, as you learn *how* these 22 amazing women turned their pain into joy. I believe you will be inspired by these motivating, inspirational, and captivating stories.

If we could do it, so can you!

All Glory to God,

~ Linda Laird Staszewski

We would all appreciate it if you could share your positive comments about our book on www.Amazon.com.

Thank you and enjoy!

The Phoenix Rebirth: Unleashing the Flame within Me

Bea Baylor/Overcomer

"Let the flames shine as a bold beacon of light, guiding you out of the depths of darkness."

~ Bea Baylor

Sometimes in life, we face challenges that leave us feeling like we've hit rock bottom, but moments allow us to rise higher and stronger than ever before. So, let's embrace the heat, channel our inner flames, and emerge from the ashes like a phoenix, ready to take on the world!

This chapter showcases the profound impact a fire can have on your life. My own experiences attest to this fact, and I am eager to share my transformational story with you. I hope discovering how I overcame challenges and adversity in my own life inspires change in yours. As I embark on a lifelong quest to extinguish the destructive flames that challenge me, I am committed to fight against whatever hinders my progress and strive to restore peace and balance in my life.

Come with me on a journey and explore how I turned my mess into my message. Rising like the phoenix from the ashes, I found my own flame through God and rebuilt my life after going through multiple traumatic events that shook the core of my soul.

When I was seven, I thought I'd burned down my family's home. I wish that was the worst of it, but there was something even more insidious lurking in the shadows: my sister and I were placed in a segregated special education program in 1965, without my parents' knowledge, because we were the only black kids in the entire school. Countless challenges followed throughout my life, including two marriages and subsequent divorces, the wrongful conviction and incarceration of my pregnant daughter, and my own diagnosis of stage III breast cancer in February 2001. Despite these struggles, my story is one of resilience and love. In June 2000, I welcomed my first grandson, Craig Griffin, into the world while his mother was in prison, and for the next 18 years, my mom and I both raised him as our own until his mom was released after spending 10 years in prison. On September 14, 2020, I successfully triumphed over two heart attacks and underwent an emergency quadruple bypass surgery during the pandemic.

Now, I am a proud survivor and live to tell my story. My experiences have only made me stronger and more determined to help others who face similar obstacles. I believe my personal life experiences are the key to achieving a better life. My message of hope, perseverance, and unwavering strength has emerged from my mess like a phoenix rising from the ashes. Its power knows no bounds. I am delighted to have you accompany me on this exciting journey as we embark on this chapter together.

Have you ever wondered why things have to be so difficult in life? Have you ever felt as if the things that you desire are far beyond your reach?

Take a moment to reflect on your life and the challenges that you've faced. I have certainly felt that way, and yet, with faith, perseverance, and vulnerability, I have found my way to a better place. Just as a phoenix rises from its ashes to become even more resplendent, I have achieved heights and successes beyond my own imagining.

Faith: Complete trust and confidence that the change I was looking for was absolutely possible.

Perseverance: Taking consistent action, even when success was delayed.

Vulnerability: A willingness to expose myself, even at the risk of being ridiculed.

I had to get intimate with these terms, applying them over and over again until complete transformation occurred

In this chapter, we will delve deeper into the origins and significance of the mythical phoenix and how its story reflects my own. Who would have thought a fire that happened when I was a little girl would define my life as a phoenix—a fire that impacted my entire life for a decade. I remembered vividly the events that took place while I was a little girl. We had wood stoves throughout the house to keep warm and an old kerosene stove to cook our food. My mother was a stay-at-home mom and loved taking care of all six of her children.

In the evenings, my mother would heat a large kettle of water atop the wood stove, so my siblings and I could take our baths. We'd wait for her to pour the warm water into a galvanized tub; then, we would take turns splashing and playing around. We loved the warm water; it always felt good to our bodies, and we loved the special time with my mother.

After our baths, we eagerly awaited Dad's arrival home. Standing close to the warm wood stove in our pajamas, we'd excitedly scan the dark road for signs of his approach. Then, a glimmer of light in the distance would signal his arrival, and we'd rush toward the gate to greet him. In those joyous moments, all we craved was his hugs and kisses. After a round of group embraces, Dad would delve into his bag of goodies, doling out candies as we sat around the stove, happily indulging and playing. When we'd had our fill, he would reach over to hug Mother and ask about dinner.

On this night though, things were different.

Daddy didn't want what Mother had prepared, so he decided to make liver and gravy. After he finished cooking, he tried to turn off the old kerosene stove but the flames wouldn't go out. Panicking, Daddy yelled, "Go get me some dirt! NOW!" My sister and I immediately reacted, running outside in our thin pajamas and grabbing handfuls of dirt. Running back into the house, we awaited his instructions.

He yelled to my sister Carolyn to sprinkle her dirt first. She threw her dirt over the flames but the fire did not go out completely. Now it was my turn, and being an anxious and naive seven-year-old, I could hardly wait for my turn to sprinkle the dirt on the remaining flames. But after I did, the fire ignited and grew into a full blaze that reached the ceiling of our house. I remember that scared feeling coming over my body and my heart starting to beat fast. As the flames drifted toward the ceiling, Dad sprang into action, barking orders, running, and holding his head. In the chaos, Mom quickly herded us outside to the safety of an open field and sprinted back inside to ensure Dad was unscathed. It was a close call, but thanks to our parents' quick thinking, we were all in the clear. As we huddled together in the open field, with only a blanket to shield us from the elements, fear and confusion washed over us. We heard a loud noise that sounded like an explosion, and in that moment, you could see the fear in my siblings' faces, as my heart started beating faster and tears streamed down my face.

My brother, and four sisters, looked so frightened that my older sister grabbed us and huddled us all together while telling me to stop crying. It's going to be OK, calling me by the name "Bea." I could feel the warmth from the fire as we held each other tightly and looked on to see if our mom and dad made it out of the burning house alive.

A flurry of thoughts raced through my mind as I contemplated my actions and pondered their consequences. I grappled with regret, thinking that I burned my parents' house down and taking the blame for everything. As we gazed into the darkness, a wave of relief washed over us when suddenly a glimmer of hope emerged as Mom and Dad came running toward us. Oh, you should have seen the relief on our faces! The first fire truck finally arrived on the scene, and Mom and Dad ran over to give them information about the fire. The firemen quickly began to put out the fire, and by the grace of God, we were all safe. Family and friends heard the bad news and started to arrive at the scene to carry us to safety. From that moment on, I vowed to never take anything for granted again. I made sure to show my appreciation for all the blessings in my life.

The fire reminded me that life is fleeting and can be snatched away in an instant. I will never forget the feeling of helplessness and fear that day, and I am so thankful for a second chance. Since then, it's ignited me to cherish each moment spent with family and friends and appreciate all of life's blessings. The loss of our beloved home taught me to cultivate resilience, strength, faith, and kindness. Despite other adversities, I continued to hold on to hope and positivity, counting my blessings and moving forward, grateful because things could have been much worse.

When you experience the lasting emotional impact of traumatic events, such as the aftermath of a fire, it has an effect on how you face adversity. I am igniting a flame that drives me to overcome any obstacle I face in the future. That's why I'm dedicated to helping women who faced similar hardships by connecting them with necessary resources. I believe that no one should suffer alone, and so I strive to ensure that everyone has access to the support they need and can find the opportunities within challenges.

During all of my difficult times, and the emotions that I experienced, my family and God provided me with much-needed support and solace. The experience has shaped who I am today and imparted valuable lessons. In all adversity, there is opportunity to break free from *what is* and begin to learn and grow.

Following the fire, my life threw more traumatic events my way, but, like the phoenix, I rose from the ashes each time. Life can be challenging and unfair—there's no denying that—however, I firmly believe with the right support, anyone can navigate their way through difficult situations. In my work, I'm deeply committed to helping those facing daunting challenges by equipping them with the tools they need to confront those challenges confidently.

The phoenix, a timeless symbol of rebirth and resilience, challenges us to face life's obstacles head-on and find strength in our trials. It's important to acknowledge that tough times will inevitably occur, but during these moments, we have the chance to bring out our very best. Don't give up!

My personal account of the phoenix's rebirth highlights a crucial life lesson: life is a never-ending journey of highs and lows, but hope prevails when we trust in our abilities to rise again.

It's a timeless story that can inspire us and keep us motivated as we face our own struggles. So, don't forget to take this story with you the next time you need a boost of motivation and courage! No matter what challenges are thrown your way, remember that you have the power to rise from them like the phoenix, reborn and even stronger than before.

Another very important aspect of my resilience and strength is my relationship with God. I would like to emphasize the importance of aspiring to a closer relationship with him. Allow the flame within you to burn bright and be a guiding light in your life, symbolizing resilience, hope, and strength. Even in the face of adversity and hardship, we can grow and transform through the ashes of our struggles.

The Rebirth of the Phoenix is a powerful message that reminds us our struggles don't have to define us! ✸

About Bea

Founded in 2014 by CEO Bea Baylor, Bea Baylor Coaching and Marketing Agency is an innovative business that has helped more than 70 nonprofits and eight small businesses, now billing over two million dollars.

Bea offers entrepreneurs a comprehensive package including business coaching, travel agency services, and podcasting.

Her mission is to help them fulfill their potential while exploring the beauty of the world. Her wealth of experience, success, and expertise in business and travel render Bea a valuable mentor for aspiring business leaders. Look out for the newest offering from her venture, Blue Sapphire Travel Agency, launched in May 2023. Bea's bespoke luxury packages cater to each traveler's unique needs, enabling everyone to embark on an unforgettable journey.

These ventures offer busy entrepreneurs a chance to escape the everyday hustle and enjoy luxurious getaways, all while continuing to run their business. Bea and her team are committed to empowering clients to find creative solutions for building successful businesses while also taking time out to travel, relax, and enjoy life. Their unique value proposition combines personalized coaching services with dynamic marketing strategies, helping entrepreneurs to embrace success in all aspects of life: financial, physical, mental, and emotional wellbeing.

Bea Baylor is the host of *The Luxury Lifestyle Blueprint Podcast*, powered by VoiceAmerica. Join her on an insightful journey through entrepreneurship, high-performance coaching, and the luxury life of modern-day entrepreneurs with weekly episodes featuring influential guests from around the globe.

Amidst the pandemic health crisis, Bea suffered a major heart attack that required open-heart surgery. Her unwavering determination prevailed, as she made a remarkable recovery. Now, she is on a mission to empower other women by showing them how to stay in business without letting it consume their lives.

Connect with Bea

Email: beabaylor@gmail.com

Facebook: https://www.facebook.com/businesscoachbaylor

LinkedIn: https://www.linkedin.com/in/bea-baylor-77aa932a/

Publication: Bea Baylor PHENOMENAL OVERCOMER® Magazine now on Amazon

Podcast: The Luxury Lifestyle - With Host Bea Baylor On Her SheReigns & SheHeals Podcast
https://www.voiceamerica.com/show/4173/the-luxury-lifestyle-with-host-bea-baylor-on-her-shereigns-and-sheheals-podcast

Travel Lifestyle Membership
https://www.xipworks.com/63014/evite

Scan QR Code for Travel Concierge Specialist

How I Used Gratitude to Change My Life!

Inez Bracy

"Nothing beats a failure but a try."[2]

-R.J. Smith

Growing up on a farm in North Carolina, the sixth of seven children, allowed me the freedom to play outside, run after my brother (the fifth child) through the cow pasture, climb trees I wasn't supposed to, and just enjoy being the best tomboy I could!

My brother hated it when I followed him around and would often run and leave me. I would run to the house crying, telling on him to Mama.

Daddy and Mama gave us strict rules on what we could and couldn't do, as well as where we could go. Mind you, we only had the *whole* outdoors as our playground, except going to the river, climbing trees, and pestering the cows.

We had several different fruit trees and were forbidden to climb them. One day, while following my brother, he looked up into the apple tree and saw this big red apple. He dared me to climb the tree to get it, and, of course, I accepted the dare.

Climbing up wasn't easy, but I had to show him I could do it. As soon as I got on the limb and reached for the apple, a snake

[2] R.J. Smith, Quote by R.J. Smith: "Nothing beats a failure but a try." | Goodreads

was crawling toward it. I jumped out of the tree, and we ran home screaming.

Mama looked out the door to see what was the matter. My brother blurted out, “Toye climbed the apple tree and saw a snake!”

Mama shook her head and finger at us. All she said was, “It’s a good thing the snake didn’t bite you, and you didn’t break any limbs.” She closed the door and went back inside.

That day was the turning point in my life. I became the girliest girl you have ever seen!

I no longer followed my brother; instead, I would hang around the house reading or playing in the yard close to the house.

I think he missed being pestered by me. He didn’t seem to have as much fun now that he didn’t have me following him all the time. Sometimes, he would come back early from exploring and playing with the animals to play with me in the yard.

Reflecting on this chain of events made me think of how blessed and deeply grateful I am for living in a time when I had the space, freedom, and guidance to be uniquely me.

I started using gratitude at a young age to change my life. Often, I would be thankful for the things I wanted as if they were already here. Many of my dreams were based on the books I read that gave me a glimpse into what life could be like.

During one stage, I dreamed I was a ballerina! I would walk around the house on my tiptoes mimicking the ballerinas I had seen on TV. Sometimes, Daddy would lift me up as if he were my dance partner, twirl me around, and then gently put me down.

Daddy was amazing. I really thought I was dancing!

I never studied to be a ballerina but admire the hard work and dedication dancers have to the art form. I love the way they make each movement seem easy and effortless.

Growing up, my parents taught us to *choose* to be grateful for all things. Even when it looked as if there was *no good* in it, we were taught to be grateful and always look for the lesson.

Remembering the lessons from my parents, I choose to be grateful regularly, to practice making decisions, creating a plan, and taking action. Just this subtle shift in my thinking causes me to feel better and get moving. Living in gratitude is a conscious decision, and being able to choose my attitude each day is one of the most important ways I can practice this mindset.

Many years ago, a mentor taught me that one way to express gratitude is to find joy in something daily and celebrate it. Some days are easier than others to create a celebration, especially when it seems as if all has gone wrong. On those days, I choose one thing, examine it, and celebrate the opportunity for me to see and feel the energy differently.

It doesn't matter how you choose to celebrate, what matters is that you do something to show appreciation for what is, what was, and what's to come. My celebrations can be as simple as looking out the window and noticing a squirrel gathering nuts, walking outside gazing at the ever-changing sky, enjoying my favorite beverage, or listening to an Audible book while preparing dinner.

Living in gratitude allows me to find the gift in all that is and all that was. Finding the gift requires attention, intention, and mindfulness. One way to do this is to intentionally look for and focus on the things—no matter how small—that cause me to smile, make my heart sing, and bring me exquisite joy.

The gift can be as humble as watching a butterfly or as bold as treating myself to that long-awaited trip.

Making gratitude a way of life energizes the Universe to deliver every valuable thing this earth offers and everything our hearts earnestly desire. For me, gratitude is more than just saying, *Thank you.* It is a mindset that allows me to focus on the positive aspects of my life, even in the face of disguised opportunities. It requires recognizing the good I have, as well as expressing appreciation, and acknowledging the efforts of others. Gratitude shifts my perspective from what is lacking to what is present, creating a sense of contentment and fulfillment.

Here are nine strategies I use to ignite my fire for living in gratitude and changing my life.

1. **Keep a gratitude journal.** It's amazing how keeping a journal helps me stay on track, sparking an attitude of gratitude. Writing at least three things daily for which I am grateful, while noticing how I feel, supports me in this practice. Making a habit of gratitude-journaling helps me become more resilient to stress and hardship. Through these practices, I have developed a stronger awareness of what I have.
2. **Smile more.** There is something magical in sharing a smile with loved ones and strangers. It is a no-cost gift that brightens your day and that of the person receiving the smile.
3. **Count my blessings**. Blessings come in many ways. I look for the hidden blessings all around me. I say *hidden* because they are sometimes very subtle, causing me to be more mindful, more aware. Saying a blessing over your food is a start.
4. **Open to the sun.** Each morning when the sun is shining, I go outside and lift my face and my arms to the sun, feeling the warmth and being grateful for it.
5. **Find three things of beauty.** While on my daily walk, I look for three things of beauty to brighten my day and count my blessings.
6. **Enjoy my morning coffee.** There's nothing quite like a fresh cup of coffee in the morning. I start by grinding

organic beans, place the grinds in a coffee press for four to five minutes, press down, and pour into my favorite cup. While preparing this coffee, I am in deepest gratitude for the farmers and all those whose work allows me to have this exquisite experience.

7. **Express appreciation.** I intentionally take the time to express gratitude to others. A simple *thank you* or a heartfelt note can go a long way in strengthening relationships and spreading positivity.
8. **Engage in mindful reflection.** Pausing and reflecting on the good things that happened during the day supports me in appreciating the small moments and finding joy in the present.
9. **Practice acts of kindness.** I love giving a sincere compliment or a smile to someone. Often, I'll hear, *Thank you. You've made my day.* By helping and supporting others, I not only make a positive impact on their lives but also cultivate a sense of gratitude within myself.

These strategies can provide an opportunity for you to take a step back, appreciate what you have, and reflect on the beauty of life. A regular practice of gratitude can help you celebrate your successes, gain perspective on difficult situations, and refocus your attention away from negative thinking. Appreciation also allows you to recognize the positive in any situation, leading to feelings of contentment, joy, and overall better health.

Additional Benefits of Practicing Gratitude

Practicing gratitude has tremendous benefits for my mental, emotional, and physical well-being by calming my mind, body, and spirit. At the same time, it also energizes and rejuvenates my body, heals my soul, restores my health, and enhances my creativity. Being grateful doesn't mean ignoring or denying challenges I face; it is about finding the silver lining and focusing on the positive aspects, even in difficult times. Practicing this gives me strength to be resilient and helps me develop a positive outlook on life.

Being grateful helps to reduce stress, improve sleep quality, and enhances my overall joy. Exercising mindfulness, attention, and intention encourages me to establish stronger relationships bringing a sense of connection and appreciation. I've also found that gratitude increases my resilience, optimism, and self-esteem. Living in gratitude opens me to opportunities that were previously not seen. Using these proven strategies helps to ensure that I stay grounded and enjoy living.

Gratitude is the most powerful tool that I use to transform my life. Intentionally cultivating a mindset of gratitude requires conscious effort and consistency, but the rewards are worth it! So, I invite you to join me in embracing gratitude and unlocking its magic to create a more fulfilling and positive life.

About Inez

Inez Bracy is a passionate, highly experienced health, wellness, and transformation coach. She has made it her life's mission to help people transform their lives by adopting healthy habits, achieving their weight release goals, and improving their overall well-being. With more than 23 years of experience in the industry, she has helped countless people overcome their struggles.

Inez has a deep understanding of the physical, mental, and emotional aspects of health and takes a holistic approach to wellness.

Getting healthy is not a marathon nor a sprint; it takes time.

Clients using Inez's proprietary processes are able to identify the underlying causes of their health challenges. They receive personalized coaching and a health/life plan addressing their unique needs. Following this plan, her clients experience results they can maintain throughout life.

Through one-on-one and group coaching, workshops, and online resources, her clients receive expert guidance on everything from nutrition and exercise to mindfulness and stress management.

Using her warm, compassionate approach, she is a trusted confidante to her clients, offering unwavering support and encouragement as they navigate their health journeys.

Whether you are looking to release weight, reduce stress, or simply improve your overall health, Inez will help you achieve your goals and thrive in every aspect of your life.

Connect with Inez

Email: inez@inezbracy.com

Website: https://inezbracy.com

Facebook: https://facebook.com/inezbracy1

From Trauma to Truth

Rachelle Bryant

"She comprehended the perversity of life, that in the struggle lies the joy."[3]

~ Maya Angelou

Disassociation made my life feel like a movie rather than reality. It was how I coped, so I could survive. My story is about how I survived the ongoing trauma that defined my life for many years and learned to live in my truth.

My father had already abandoned one family, including two children. He was an alcoholic and a narcissist. My mother had been married once, struggled with issues from being adopted, was addicted to cigarettes, and had narcissistic tendencies.

I was born a week late on Fairfax, Va.'s, hottest day in 1978. I refused to come out. Perhaps the nine-month diet of cigarettes and feeling my mom's worry about losing me after a stillborn baby the year before, made the thought of the outside world seem even scarier. After a vacuum, forceps, and a lot of pulling, I was born.

That day, the umbilical cord was cut, but a new cord was formed—the trauma bond.

A narcissistic mother is terrified of, and yet dependent on, the attachment of another human being. For her, I was that person. My mom would tell me, "I had you because I wanted someone

---

[3] Maya Angelou, Quote by Maya Angelou: "She comprehended the perversity of life, that i..." | Goodreads

who had to love me because we are biologically related." Though I loved my mom, this statement created a huge responsibility that would stunt the healthy boundaries I needed to set with her and other adults. Trying to live up to her standards, trying to be *good enough,* was my future.

I tried to meet and exceed her expectations my entire life, but a narcissist can never be satisfied. The bar was just raised higher and higher.

Trauma

When I was two or three, my dad and I spent a typical morning watching the birds outside when something new happened: my dad collapsed. I found my mom and told her in toddler words, "Daddy went back to sleep."

My dad died that morning, and my mom brought him back several times before the paramedics arrived. He survived three brain aneurysms that day. He later resented my mom for saving his life because he was never the same.

While my dad was in the hospital, our neighbors took me to a restaurant where I had an accident. I fell onto a bamboo table, slicing my face open. When I arrived at the emergency room, my mom told me that she couldn't handle the stress of her child and husband being *sick* at the same time. She chose her husband, who wasn't even aware of her presence, to avoid the screaming child who had just busted her face open.

She left me alone.

About two years later, the man she chose to comfort over the needs of her child, became violent from not taking his meds. He took a gun and said he didn't know which one of us to kill first so the other could watch. Thankfully, my mom helped him de-escalate, and our neighbor took his guns away. We fled soon after that, moved in with my grandparents, and my parents divorced.

That was it—no more Daddy.

Trauma

At seven years old, my second-grade art class got to play with clay. I could make a mug, vase, ashtray, or basket. I chose a basket because it was the hardest. I loved a challenge, constantly raising my own bar and hoping for positive attention from my mom.

When it came time to paint it, I looked at all the colors. Which one would make my basket perfect? The reds and blues were popular. Green was almost gone. Yellow and purple were popular too. I knew better than to use orange. My mom hated that color, and it was never allowed.

I looked at brown, and no one had touched it. It looked lonely and sad that no one had included it in their masterpieces. I decided it needed a purpose, and it would feel better if I chose it as the color for my fantastic piece. I hoped my mom would always treasure it.

Instead of being cherished and getting positive attention, it landed me in therapy. My teachers thought it reflected my sadness because my parents were divorced, and I didn't ever see my dad. That one decision led me to my first experience with sexual abuse at the hands of my therapist.

I don't regret giving brown a chance to shine with my piece of art, but I wish the adults in my life would have listened to how proud I was and why I chose brown. Instead, they came to their own conclusions. What was innocent and beautiful became an awful experience that would set me up for more trauma.

My mom kept the basket until she died in 2021. Then, I became the owner. I'm not sure if she treasured it or if it represented something else for her. She never knew about what happened between me and my therapist. One day, when we came in for therapy, he was gone, and no one gave us any details of where he moved or why. Sometimes I wonder if she knew, and the basket reminded her of that awful decision, but I will never know.

The basket now sits on my desk as a reminder of the innocence of seven-year-old me. What happened at that age forever changed me in ways that I am just now realizing at age 44.

Trauma

At age nine, my mom moved me to Texas to live with the love of her life. She forced me to leave everything I knew in Virginia. Little did I know, I would leave my identity there as well. Something I have been struggling to find ever since.

He was Catholic, and we were Jewish. For them to have any chance to get married, she had to become Catholic and have me convert as well. Converting meant everything I was, understood, and believed would be taken from me.

My mom told me to lie to my grandparents because if they ever found out about our lives as Catholics, they would disown us, and it would be my fault. It was another lie, but I was just a kid, and I was supposed to trust my parents. My grandparents were my only safe place; my constant for stability and unconditional love. They would never have blamed me for my mom's decisions, but I was scared, so I lied. It tore me apart each time.

I hated every part of my double life. I felt alone, isolated, and confused. Anything, or anyone, who reminded me of my life before Texas felt good and comforting.

When my parents met my future godfather, and we found out he was from New York, I thought I had found my connection back to a piece of myself that had been missing. He was the liturgist of our church, and I quickly became his *special* helper. He became family to us, and my parents grew to love him more and more. When he needed a place to stay for a while, before buying a house, my parents invited him to stay with us.

For years, he groomed me and my parents by befriending us. We didn't know it, but it was a common thing for molesters to do.

I lived with my rapist at the invitation of my parents. My parents caught him exposing himself a few times, and he always talked my parents out of seeing it for what it was, which only made his power over me greater.

The first time I tried to tell my mom after he had moved out, she blew it off and said I was overreacting. My parents were about to leave for Australia for two weeks, and all she could think of was how I was inconveniencing her because he was supposed to be my guardian while they were gone. So, I dropped it and stayed with friends so as to not put her out.

My parents later said they tried to resolve it by going to the diocese, but nothing happened. He kept his job at the church and was allowed near other kids.

Years later, I told the cops, which resulted in my molester only getting a five-year prison sentence, the dividing of our church into those who believed me and those who didn't, an exposed diocese that knew what happened and tried to cover it up, and two parents who blamed me for causing stress in their marriage.

I went through two trials alone. One time after testifying, I was on the ground crying when my parents started yelling at me to the point that the district attorney asked that they never be allowed near me again. I was appointed a police officer to protect me.

Trauma

When I was 23 years old, my parents divorced. My mom blamed me in a 15-page handwritten note stating that exposing my truth hurt her marriage to my stepfather. My childhood had a central theme: adults not taking responsibility for their actions and holding a child responsible in the most harmful ways.

Trauma to Truth

No matter what parts make up our stories, we can choose whether to allow them to destroy us or claim victory and use them to support others.

Many speak about generational curses or things running in the family, but from an early age, I knew I would end the ones that ran in my family. I would be nothing like them and would raise my children differently.

I have given into despair. I have wanted to give up. The weight of having family secrets is too much even for the strongest person to bear.

The events that happened to me were not a choice and often left me feeling powerless. Still, my greatest superpower was giving my pain purpose by supporting others.

My faith in God, and in myself, has given me the greatest joy—something no one can take from me.

Mental health matters.

You matter.

"Whatever tugs at your soul are the parts of your story. It's there for a reason and to be shared. Let your spirit ignite and shine your light into the world that's full of others craving to bask in it."

~ Rachelle Bryant

About Rachelle

Rachelle Bryant is a speaker, author, advocate, and entrepreneur, focusing on breaking the stigma of mental health. She has had to find her way to keep going throughout life's challenges. Many circumstances tried to distract and derail her. Still, she has walked the walk and proudly lives her authentic life. She received a life-saving kidney transplant in August 2020. It was during the pandemic, but that didn't stop her! It only grew her determination to thrive stronger and share with others that pain has a purpose, and everyone can live an unstoppable, authentic life.

Connect with Rachelle

Email: rachelle@wildlyfreellc.com

Facebook: www.facebook.com/rachelle.bryant.7

Facebook Group:
www.facebook.com/groups/mentalhealthmattersgroup/

Instagram: www.instagram.com/coloradobryant6

Website: www.WildlyFreeLLC.com

Five-Ton Watermelon

Pam Vogt Duffin

"Transformation is a process. I know that even now I will stumble and fall from time to time, but because of God's grace, I will get back up and continue on."

~ Pam Vogt Duffin

I can still feel my fingers in my throat, reaching farther and farther back until they hit that spot and the expulsion began. I remember my face afterward: the bulging eyes and broken blood vessels. How ironic. In my mind, I was doing this to be prettier. Talk about your ill-favored addictions—I would have preferred to say I was an alcoholic or drug addict because saying my vice was food made me feel like even more of a loser. I wasted 13 years of my life being insecure, unhappy, and hating myself.

It all began when I was a chubby little girl in the fifth grade at a new school, and the kids bullied me, calling me names like "five-ton watermelon" and "ocean liner." One classmate wrote in my yearbook, "Dear Pam, You're not an ocean liner, you're a steamboat." Kids can be so cruel and have no idea the lifelong scars they inflict! Because of this, one Monday, instead of buying my weekly lunch ticket, I bought a pint size carton of milk—nothing else—and my nightmare began.

Unbeknownst to the bullies, I didn't need their wrath to bring me down; I was already there. My mom was an alcoholic, and fourth grade had already put me over the edge. We moved but were still attending our old school so my sister Audrey could finish eighth grade there. The school was far from our new home. Audrey and I would sit outside of school for hours waiting for

Mom to pick us up. Eventually, the blue Nova would come speeding up to the school. I remember lying in the back seat crying the whole way home because I was so afraid we would get in an accident and be seriously injured or killed. Glenwood Park Avenue was a road we took on our way home, and there was a cliff with no guard rail.

One day, as I lay afraid in the backseat, I heard Audrey scream and I peeked up just in time to see the car veering toward the cliff. Audrey grabbed the steering wheel and turned it the other way; she saved our lives. Then there was the time my mom disappeared for the afternoon, and when the blue Nova finally pulled in the driveway, it didn't stop, despite my sister Kathy, being directly in its path. I watched in horror, thinking Kathy would be pinned between the car and the garage door. My dad managed to open the car door, and as my mom started to fall out, he stopped the car.

Years of therapy would teach me that I couldn't control my mom's drinking, but I learned that I could control my weight. So, I focused all my energy there in the unhealthiest way possible.

After the carton of milk didn't cut it anymore, I used the Ayds diet supplement which was a popular caramel appetite suppressant candy in the 1970s. You ate the caramel and then drank a warm beverage, making the supplement expand in your stomach so you'd feel full and not eat. From the end of the sixth grade to the beginning of seventh, I lost a lot of weight and *voila!* In seventh grade, I was popular, which only ingrained in me the need to be skinny to be loved. I rarely ever ate in high school and I became addicted to speed, which was an illegal weight loss drug. I thought if I was skinny enough and pretty enough everyone would love me. The irony of the eating disorder is that I was skinny—I wore a size seven in high school—but in my eyes, I was fat, ugly, and unlovable.

As young children, we're so vulnerable that any baggage from a parents' divorce, abuse, or addiction in the family can trigger insecurity. Whatever the deep emotional scar is that sets you off on the path to self-destruction, the bottom line is, *get help!* You must deal with the problem. Nothing—not alcohol, drugs, sex, or food—will make it disappear. The addiction is merely a diversion, and you'll wake up one day, perhaps years later, a miserable addict of some sort with the same deep-seated scar still gnawing at you from the inside out.

When I was 21, I married my boyfriend who had often cheated on me. I blamed it on my weight even though I was thin, which just made things worse. At that point, whenever I did eat, I'd either throw up afterward or eat a box of Ex-Lax like it was a Hershey's bar. I became a totally different person—mentally, as well as physically—shutting myself off from those who loved me and engulfed in a struggle of self-hate and perfectionism.

Finally, I couldn't take it anymore. I was so sick of thinking about what I could and couldn't eat and sneaking off to the bathroom to purge if I did, that I went to see a psychiatrist. This was before anorexia nervosa and bulimia were recognized as eating disorders, so confessing my issues was humiliating. I felt like a freak.

I wound up at the Center for Overcoming Problem Eating (COPE) Unit at Western Psych in Pittsburgh. It wasn't a camp or spa like they have now to deal with these issues. It was a lock-down unit in a psychiatric hospital. You'd occasionally hear screaming from other wards, or the alarm that would go off if someone needed to be restrained. It was scary to say the least. Plus, when you've spent so many years not eating, throwing-up, and taking laxatives, your digestive system doesn't work. When you're forced to eat, it's very uncomfortable, and when you went to the bathroom at COPE, you'd have someone standing in front of you watching you on the toilet to make sure you didn't throw up. Back then, they didn't have drugs to help you get off the drugs you were addicted to either, so add in the withdrawals from the speed ... and welcome to the necessary rock-bottom.

I vividly remember two other patients: one was a young girl a couple of years older than I was when I started down this road (around age 11), and the other, an older woman probably in her 50s, like I am now. The young lady kept saying if she would lose five more pounds, then she could eat. She was so angry that her family found out and put her in Western Psych. She couldn't understand why I wished someone would've known about me and done the same. The older woman had suffered from this disease since she was young. Both patients had to be hooked up to IVs to keep them alive.

I wound up with erosion of my esophagus, tooth enamel and gums, immune disorders, a hiatal hernia, and a rectal prolapse: issues that would last a lifetime. All this just to fit into a size five? No, it was about much more!

Here are some truths about addiction:

- Alcoholics and drug addicts don't drink or use drugs just for the buzz.
- People addicted to porn don't just like to view naked bodies.
- Gambling addicts don't just want to win money.
- My dad didn't smoke two packs of non-filtered Pall Malls a day because he liked the taste of burning tobacco.

We're all just trying to fill a hole left by someone or something, numb the pain, and erase the bad memories! And we don't always overcome our addiction one hundred percent. When I was watching my dad suffer and die from lung cancer, my eating disorder resurfaced—go figure—because it was never about being skinny; it was about avoiding the real issues that hurt and scared me. These were things I couldn't do anything about.

My mom was also stuffing down bad memories as her dad was an alcoholic and would beat her mom when he was drunk. Her brother became an alcoholic, and he died from his addiction. My mom loved us very much, took care of us, and was the best mother she knew how to be despite her alcoholism, which she did eventually overcome.

If you have children or grandchildren, please be aware of and take swift action against any teasing or bullying. You never know what's going on in a child's mind; what they might be thinking about how they *can* and *should* fix themselves.

My mom would say, "There's a place in the heart that will never be happy," but I've learned that a lot of addictions stem from our own fears and insecurities. We stuff our feelings to avoid dealing with the real issues, and that steals our happiness. We need to allow ourselves to feel the emotions, to face and work through the problems, and to ask others for help when we need it.

I am happy to say that, during my stay at the COPE Unit, I did the work and came out of there with my head together concerning my eating disorders and unhealthy relationships, which also helped me to end that bad marriage. I no longer see myself as fat or starve myself or throw up after I eat or take laxatives. I take care of myself by eating right, most of the time. We all splurge once in a while, and that's OK. I make sure to get daily exercise with either a cardio, weight training, or yoga workout. We also walk our dogs daily; they need daily exercise too! I've been happily married since 2006 to Greg, a wonderful man and my best friend!

I'm thankful for The Coffee Club Divas group. We share our faith in God and our accomplishments (as well as our failures), and we truly want to help each other succeed both personally and professionally.

Transformation is a process. I know that, even now, I will stumble and fall from time to time, but because of God's grace, I will get back up and continue on.

In contrast to my mom's old saying, I say, "There's a place in our hearts that only God can fill." And I pray we all let him do that.

God bless you all with a healthy, happy, and peaceful life!

About Pam

(Left) 5th grade—when I was called "ocean liner" and "steamboat"

(Right) High school graduation, age 17, the tank top is actually a child's size 6 undershirt

Pam Vogt Duffin is from Erie, Pa., and has been writing poetry, prose, and prayers since fourth grade. Her work has been published in *The Asylum,* Gannon University's literary magazine, and *The Erie Times.* Pam believes if we endure and overcome trauma, we should use our experiences to help others and that faith in God is key. Pam is the office manager of information technology services at Gannon University where she has worked for 27 years. She loves spending time with her husband and dogs at home, hiking, and relaxing at camp.

Connect with Pam

Email: p.duffin@yahoo.com

Facebook: www.facebook.com/pvogtduffin

Nothing Can Fill the Hole ... But Jesus

Tammy Lyn Fox, Mother to the Nations

"O taste and see that the Lord is good, Blessed is the man or woman that Trusted in Him."

~ Psalm 34:8

This is how it all began for me. I am the eldest of four children in our family. I just celebrated my 57th birthday! It is an absolute miracle and gift from God that I am alive!

I was born in Ridgway, Pa., down the middle of the state in the gorgeous, rich mountains of the Allegheny National Forest. Shortly after, my parents and I relocated to Erie. My father wanted to provide good support for us, as the coal mines were all closing down back home, so that's where we landed.

Life growing up in my parents' house was tough. We had more rules and regulations than you could imagine. I never felt loved by my mother and was physically abused until I left at age 18. My two brothers were born eight years apart, and my mom had a rough time after the youngest was born. The beatings got worse. She hit my father as well. Flipped dressers, smashed televisions ... and the list goes on. I lived in a constant state of fear. And nothing I ever did was quite good enough for her.

That root of rejection started early in my life, and I didn't even realize it.

Mom was much closer to my sister, and I couldn't understand why. Then the truth came out when my sister and I were in high school. I never even knew until I was a teenager what had happened.

About seven months after I was born, my mother began working as a cocktail waitress in a local spot named Strubbe's. She got a taste of the city life and met another man to fill the hole deep in her heart. She left me and my father. I was just a baby.

When she realized that this "new man" was a useless drunk and would never be able to take care of her, she returned home to me and my father. She was pregnant by the other man. My father, being the loving supportive husband, said he would raise that child as his own, and he did.

As we were growing up, we were involved with our church and youth group. More rules & regulations when I just wanted love. I found myself looking for validation. Love in all the wrong places, as you would say! I had boyfriends from a youth group and boys from school, which got me into trouble with my mom. My father tried to be the peacemaker in our house, but it just didn't work. I remember him crying and begging my mother to stop the wrath when she was upset with me.

My only solace was summertime. I was allowed to go back to Ridgway and stay with my great-grandfather. I called him "Pappy," and I adored him. My Pappy died of cancer when I was 16. It broke my heart.

Shortly after that, I dabbled in drugs and alcohol to "fill the hole" and numb the pain. That sent me in a different direction completely. I left home and the church at age 18. I ran away from my pain and problems. I lived in Florida several times and then California, but even with all that running, I realized I needed help. I desperately wanted to be whole. I started dating a lawyer at one point, and we had a nice house with a maid. I couldn't please him either, though. I lost my only pregnancy ever due to miscarriage when he and I were considering a split.

Failure. Rejection. They followed me everywhere. And then six months after our divorce, when I was 28, my father died of cancer.

I wanted to die. I was so angry at God because he didn't take *her*—my mother—instead. My life spiraled for two years.

I moved to Tucson, Ariz., and just disappeared. On the week of my 30th birthday I ended up in jail. It saved my life. Divine intervention. Eleven days later, my mother came to get me and bring me home. It was the first time I ever felt love from her in my life.

It has been a long 27 years of healing, but I can say that we are now friends. You really set yourself free when you do the heart work and release people with forgiveness. I rededicated my heart to God that summer and started the journey of forgiving myself and my mother and restoring many relationships. It was through that forgiveness that I saw a glimpse of what real love and relationships look like. Even Christ, while being led to the cross for crucifixion said, "Father, forgive them; for they know not what they do." (Luke 23:34-38 NIV) I realized that my mother was doing the best she could, even though it may not have looked like it when I was growing up. Pieces of her love came through in all the rules. She cared, though she didn't know how to show it.

I have realized that nothing else will satisfy a person. Only God can make me whole and fill the hole inside of me. There is a cavity in our spirit that we search the whole world to fill through work, relationships, shopping, drugs, alcohol, exercise, etc.

I am finally learning to say "no," to set boundaries, and avoid perfectionism (getting there!), which only leads to procrastination and self-sabotage. I realize what I bring to the table and value it. I don't settle for poor relationships, because peace is priceless to me today.

I want to close with one of my favorite scriptures from the Holy Bible!

> Sing, O barren one though that didst not bear, break forth into singing and cry out loud, thou that didst not travail with child: for more are the children of the desolate than the children of the married wife, saith the Lord. Enlarge the place of thy tent and let them stretch forth the curtains of thine habitations; spare not, lengthen thy cords, strengthen thy stakes; for thou shalt break forth on the right hand and on the left; and thy seed shall inherit the Gentiles and make the desolate cities to be inhabited. Fear Not; for thou shalt not be ashamed: neither be though confounded; for though shalt not be put to shame: for thou shalt FORGET the shame of thy youth, and shalt not remember the reproach of thy widowhood anymore. (Isahiah 54:1-4)

I am so grateful to God for his restoration in my life. He has blessed me with two beautiful sons from Nigeria; both of whom are married, have wonderful careers, and have recently given me a grandson, Gabriel, and a granddaughter, Valentina. I finally choose joy in my life on a daily basis!

He continues to amaze me!

About Tammy

Tammy Lyn Fox is a custom caterer who creates tantalizing dishes from all over the world. After developing her skills in the restaurant industry throughout the United States and Canada for 28 years, she started a catering company, "Taste of Zion" after returning home to Erie in 2006. Tammy loves to take you on a journey with waves of flavor and believes food should be an experience!

A few years later, Tammy began working at Christian Boarding. While running her business from that commercial kitchen, she held the position of head chef and Mama to 40–50 international high school students from all over the world. She taught cooking classes for Erie First Christian Academy, while celebrating every international holiday represented at the dormitory for seven years.

Since then, Tammy has been involved in mission work with Church Planting International in Peru, Uganda, Dominican Republic, Guatemala, and Jamaica. She continues to impact countless lives worldwide with her food and love of Jesus.

Presently, she is developing a nonprofit organization and blog to chronicle her food, travel, and mission work. Global Kitchen Commission will provide the best spiritual and physical nutrients to impoverished areas of the world. She hopes to inspire others to impact their communities as well.

We must take part in the bigger picture.

Connect with Tammy

Facebook - Tammy Lyn Fox

https://www.Facebook.com/tlfox2

Chef d'entreprise at Global Kitchen

Global Kitchen, 4115 West Ridge Road, Erie, Pa

https://www.Facebook.com/GlobalKitchenbytasteofzion

Proprietor at Taste of Zion Custom Catering

https://www.Facebook.com/TasteofZionCustomCatering

The Lotus

Alisa Gannon

"Just like the lotus, we too have the ability to rise from the mud, bloom out of the darkness and radiate into the world."[4]

~ Buddhist Saying (author unknown)

This quote about the lotus flower became so powerful for me that I even got a tattoo of one on my back. The muck and mire held me captive for too many years. I am working my way out and look forward to my time to shine.

How It All Began

My early childhood was uneventful. I was born in 1970 in Erie, Pa. Our family included me, Mom, Dad, and my two older brothers. Things got rough around the time I was 11. My father had been drinking too much for years, and now, he was a bottle-or-two-a-day, drop-down, stinking drunk. Imagine my horror as an awkward middle schooler when I came home into our subdivision and found him lying in the yard, moaning loudly and too drunk to get up. Or when he would fall down the stairs (again) and lay at the bottom, yelling. There were scary nights when my mom would sleep with me as he banged on the door for hours. We would put dressers in front of it to keep him from coming in.

There was no physical abuse. I didn't learn until many years later that emotional abuse hurts too. It makes me sick when I think about it now, but I just tried to get through it back then. I

---

[4]Unknown author, 20 Lotus Flower Quotes to Inspire Growth & New Beginnings– Healing Brave

begged my mother to leave my dad, but she felt she had nowhere to go. When my daughters were 11 and 14, I would tiptoe into their rooms at night to steal a hug. I would watch them sleeping peacefully and try to imagine them going through what I had at their age. I would cry because it just seemed too horrible. I also wept for my younger self and the childhood that was stolen from me.

A Family of Five Becomes a Family of Four

One seemingly ordinary afternoon in eighth grade, the cops came to our house. My grandparents were visiting, so my grandma called out to me. I went to the top of the stairs, and she said, "Your dad died in a car crash." All I could respond with was, "OK." That was all. I went to my room and felt like I would throw up. I had no idea how I felt about his death. I know I didn't react as expected. I went to the showings and funeral in a stupor, not believing that I lost my father at such a young age. The truth is, we lost him long before the accident. I didn't realize it then, but that left a big hole in my heart.

I very efficiently buried any grief I felt. I didn't realize this until many years later, but I was relieved when my father died. Then I was ashamed of how I dealt with his death. I have trouble remembering the good times, but I know they existed. My dad was brilliant. In the 1970s, he worked on massive computers at the paper mills without any formal training. Before that, he was a sergeant in the army.

That Dirty Ten-Letter Word

As a teen, I was diagnosed with depression. I began taking medications and saw counselors. It worked somewhat, but I couldn't beat it. My self-esteem was low, and I was embarrassed about my depression. I kept trudging through life, doing the best I could. I still take medications and talk to a psychologist. It gets better at times and worse at others.

I have always loved music. I joined the marching band in high school and felt more myself after each performance. As a senior, I became a drum major, which I thoroughly enjoyed. Music was the perfect escape for me.

A Family of Four Becomes a Family of Three

My brother, Mike, was just two years older than me. I looked up to him, as well as my oldest brother. Sometime in Mike's senior year, 1986, he started drinking to quell his depression. He went for rehabilitation and learned to become a mechanic. He worked for a while but fell off the wagon. Back to rehab he went. It just broke my heart. When he was sober, he was so funny, and everyone loved his laugh.

Unfortunately, in the early 2000s, his drinking got out of hand. He had been living with my older brother but was kicked out due to his antics. One day, my older brother went to check on him and found that he had spent most of the day in some dump hotel, getting drunk. He was very sick. My brother took him to the hospital, and the doctor said he had pneumonia. I was heartbroken, looking at his barely recognizable, swollen body. He died in just a few days at the age of 34. I was devastated by his death but would tuck that pain away into a place I refused to go.

Building My Own Family

On one ordinary day, while in pharmacy school, I met the love of my life, Drew. We both were working at a pizza shop. He is five years older than me, was divorced, and had custody of two young daughters. I just knew when I was around him, things were all right. And it remains that way today. He is my rock, and we are so good together. I have never seen a better father or husband than him. We always enjoy our time together. We love making day trips to fun little shops, taking vacations by the ocean, gardening, and rollerblading, whenever possible. I loved feeling so powerful whizzing along.

The Cycle Continues

We married in 1998 and had our first daughter, Quinn Marie, in 1999. Oh, how I loved her. But I was suffering from intense postpartum depression—yet another thing to make me disappointed in myself. Eventually, the postpartum depression faded into a low-level depression. Three years later, we had Paige Evelyn ... and it happened again. Even while being down, my family brought me great joy. I loved all four girls and Drew very much, but I was struggling. I didn't like my job as a pharmacist and found it stressful. I was dragging all the time. Sleep was not refreshing, and I felt like I was falling apart.

The Perfect Storm

After working for 17 years as a pharmacist, I just got up and left the hospital pharmacy on a particularly stressful day. It seems surreal now. I went to my psychiatrist and said, "Something is wrong with me." My depression was at an all-time low. It seemed like it had come out of nowhere. My doctor put my supportive husband on suicide watch over me. We quickly saw that I needed help, fast. I started going to Western Psychiatric Hospital for shock therapy. Yep, they still do that. I was so embarrassed that I had to go that route. The doctors began by putting an electrode on just one temple. They said there was less of a chance for memory loss. Luckily, they put me under anesthesia before they initiated treatment. I still woke up crying and with a bad migraine many times. We took this route for a few months. They kept increasing the dose of electricity. Then finally, they went to both temples, affecting both lobes of the brain. I wish I could say it worked, but it only made a small dent, so we quit that treatment. I began to feel hopeless.

Finally, my doctor put me on a drug they rarely use because you must watch what you eat to avoid severe hypertension. After about two weeks, I started seeing the light. I was on that medication for a few years, then was able to switch to a common antidepressant. Unfortunately, because shock therapy had affected my memory, especially long-term, returning to the pharmacy was not an option.

My Aha Moment

Then, my body turned on me. I was so tired; I had fluid on my knee and couldn't think straight. I was diagnosed with narcolepsy, fibromyalgia, and rheumatoid arthritis, among other things. What the hell was happening to me? My psychiatrist sent me to an excellent psychologist, who I still see. He said the combination of my buried grief and the high stress of my job just bubbled up and practically incapacitated me. This news blindsided me. I also learned that I had post-traumatic stress disorder (PTSD) often the catalyst for diseases such as fibromyalgia. I couldn't have been more surprised. I told him, "I don't deserve a diagnosis of PTSD. How can that compare to a soldier who saw death and destruction?" Then I would cry, feeling guilty for whining about how minimal my situation seemed in comparison. I soon learned that we all have our struggles, and there is no use in comparing them. PTSD is actually quite common in children with an alcoholic parent.

I started therapy, but I would get physically sick and cancel my appointments. It took me a month or two, but I realized I didn't want to talk to the psychologist about my dad and brother. So, we backed off it for a bit and approached it in more minor ways. I still have things to work through. Sometimes, it just hurts too much, but I'm working my way out of that mud, little by little.

Finding My Happy Place

I have dabbled in many jobs and hobbies, trying to find a purpose. I made jewelry and did some blogging and copywriting, among other things. Nothing felt quite right for me. I finally found my true calling about ten years ago. I quickly became enamored by watercolor painting, paper art, mixed media, and more.

I started journaling, which I highly recommend. Then I started making journals. The journals are interactive with flips, pockets, and more. They also often include items saved from the trash. Additionally, I make photo albums and greeting cards and play with mixed media. It is very therapeutic for me. Once I get started, it's hard for me to stop, which means I am quite the messy crafter. My husband mainly bites his tongue because he is glad I found something that brings me joy. While moving my mother in with us, I discovered photos of my father, mostly before hard times hit. I cherish these photos. I realized that I have forgiven him, but I don't think that hole in my heart will ever completely heal.

I invite joy into my life, now. I have been working at living in the moment and am slowing down, celebrating small victories. I used to need to have something to look forward to, which meant I missed all the beautiful things happening in the present. I feel blessed to have found friends, family, and activities that bring me great joy. Where am I now? You can find me by the pond, shaking off the mud, and with my face toward the sun.

About Alisa

Alisa Gannon is an author, self-taught artist, and lover of all that is messy. She graduated from Duquesne School of Pharmacy with a bachelor's degree. She has a small home-based business specializing in handmade journals, photo albums, and cards. Alisa has four lovely grown daughters and one adored granddaughter. She lives in Erie, Pa., with her husband of 25 years. You can usually find her in her studio, working on yet another project and wading through discarded projects.

Connect with Alisa

Website: www.xoalisadesigns.com

Facebook: www.facebook.com/xoalisa

Instagram: https://www.instagram.com/xoalisadesigns

Journey from Despair to Joy

Roberta Holdsworth

"There are three types of people: those who make things happen, those who watch things happen, and those who wonder what happened."[5]

~ Mary Kay Ash

I am a woman currently in my mid-50s with two grown children: one boy and one girl (ten years apart) and two grandchildren. I was a single mom for most of my children's growing years and, thus, worked multiple jobs. My story is about triumphing over a legacy of poverty and alcoholism.

My mother was the only girl among five boys. My grandfather died young, while saving my uncle who had fallen in a creek, so my grandmother was left to raise the six children on her own. My grandmother also died young from tuberculosis. My mother's family background has had a big impact on how I grew up, as you will see.

As an orphan and a girl, my mother was put in St. Joseph's Orphanage prior to being put in foster care with her youngest brother. She got married at 18 and had two boys before they separated. To avoid paying child support, their father had them taken away by child services and put in the foster care system. A few years after that, my mother had an affair with a married man. He could not claim me as his child, so I grew up as an only child.

[5] Mary Kay Ash, Quote by Mary Kay Ash: "There are three types of people in this world: ..." | Goodreads

During the time of my mother's grief and anguish, she self-medicated with alcohol and later became an alcoholic.

On the day I was born, my mother was at the bar drinking and playing pool. There were times she would have people watch me when I was too young to watch myself. Often, she would leave me with people and then forget where I was for days: some were good places, some were not. Between first and fourth grade, I was in foster care due to my mom's health issues, including over 20 surgeries prior to having her leg amputated.

I remember when I turned ten, my mother telling me, "Your double digits now. You can take care of yourself," and she was not joking. I had to get myself up for school, and when I returned home to an empty house, I had to figure out something to eat. My mother thought of this when she shopped with her food stamps, as she bought me cans of Chef Boyardee, soup, sandwich makings, and hot dogs that I could eat without having to cook. She informed me that she would provide me with a few sets of clothes for school; however, if I wanted any more than that, I had to earn the money myself. That is when I first became an entrepreneur.

I would do miscellaneous chores for people to earn money so I could buy what I needed. I would try to save up for big ticket items, but my stepfather would always steal the money. So, I got in the habit of spending whatever I had right away, which became an issue later in life.

I remember a time I begged my mother to please be home when I got home from school because I had an awesome report card and wanted to share it with her. Of course, she was not home, which made me angry, and I trashed the house.

As a preteen and teenager, I ran away multiple times, hoping that they would put me in a foster home. One time, I was missing for days, and when the police found me, my mother was at the bar ... of course. The police officer asked her, "What are you doing? Celebrating that she's gone?"

There was a time I remember being very sick and vomiting, and I went to my mother at the bar begging her to take me to the emergency room. She kept stating she would, "... after this quart of beer." Finally, my uncle (who was also drunk), said to my mother, "Give me your medical card, and I'll take her to the emergency room." My mother gave him the medical card, and my uncle took me to the hospital.

By the time I was around 13, my mother began to experience seizures whenever she drank for more than three days. So, she cut down on her drinking. At that point, my stepfather left. My mother found a new boyfriend who moved in right away. We lived in a much smaller apartment. It only had one bedroom, so my room was the living room, and my bed was the couch.

My mother would attempt to discipline me for assorted reasons, but I would ignore her. I knew that in a couple of days she would return to drinking again. I didn't feel I had to be accountable to her. Fortunately, I had a friend whose parents took me in during those awful times.

Her new boyfriend was good for a while, but then he ended up showing his true self; he was a violent person. One time, I heard muffled noises coming from their room. Opening the door, I saw him sitting on her, choking her. I was old enough that I was able to fight him to stop it. This was the first of many times. It got so bad that I started having night terrors and had to see a psychologist, who suggested I leave the situation as soon as possible. I was rarely ever home after that, and I swore no man would ever lay his hands on me and *live to regret it*.

In my early 20s, I was on the same path that my mother chose, except I worked various jobs. I would drink many evenings and weekends, to be able to fall sleep. Graced with my daughter, who was a savior to me, I swore that my children would not be raised in the bar, nor would they live on the street. This promise helped me become a better person. I joined various women groups to grow in my personal development and strengthen my courage so I could provide for my children.

I was with my son's father in my early 30s to early 40s, and he eventually became my husband. He was not a violent person, but he was an alcoholic and would steal money from me often. He would come and go; finally, his lifestyle caught up to him and he died of cancer. Although this sounds terrible, it was a godsend in many ways. He had never contributed financially, plus his constant stealing from me hindered my financial situation. When he passed, I was able to get social security to help raise my son, and things improved.

I am not saying that all times as a single mom were either easy or hard, but I was able to make sure that they were safer than my experience growing up. I did miss a lot of their childhood due to all the hours I worked. I was never good with money and was always behind on bills. However, we managed, and they turned out to be great people.

Our happy outcome is due in part to the many women I met from various groups, including Safenet (a shelter for abused women), Dress for Success, and the Coffee Club Divas. Without their love, compassion, and mentoring, I know I would not be the strong person I am today. These women made it possible for me to escape the generational trap that would have overcome me if they had not reached out their hands and hearts.

I do not regret the things that happened in my life, as they molded me into who I am today. The legacy I wish to leave is not that of money but of empowerment. I want to help empower as many women as I can. I want to let them know that they are not alone, and there are women out there who want to hold them up high, so they can be the best version of themselves.

About Roberta

Roberta Holdsworth is an administrative professional and an entrepreneur. She has two grown children and two grandchildren. She is an advocate for empowering women in various ways, including a YouTube channel that showcases successful women entrepreneurs. She has taken many self-improvement courses and has utilized life/business coaches to help with her personal development.

Connect with Roberta

Email: rlholdsworth@yahoo.com

YouTube: https://www.youtube.com/@robertasempowerium

A Prayer for Rain

Dr. Andrea Jeffress

"And it came to pass in a meanwhile,
that the heaven was black with clouds and wind,
and there was a great rain."
~ 1 Kings 18:45 (KJV)

Growing up in a home without your father present is like surviving a long drought. Every day you pray for water's saving grace. Every day you wish it would rain, and your dad would come home.

My prayer for rain was born spending summers with my God-fearing grandparents. One of my favorite childhood memories was eating a big breakfast and going to vacation Bible school. As a certified, nerdy bookworm who would go on to college at age 14, I was obsessed with the Bible stories centering around God's command over water, and its sheer power to cleanse and renew. God was the ultimate rainmaker.

After my parents divorced, my Dad left, and I prayed that he would fall from the heavens like warm summer rain and make his way home. Yet, for many years, my prayers seemed to go unanswered. Dad was like a rolling thunder cloud, threatening with lightning, but never actually raining to drench us with his love and renew our family. The drought in his absence would last for 20 years.

The Addiction

Dad was special. He always smelled sweet and fresh, like spring rain in a garden. Around town, his nickname was "Sweetwater Toulson." But even the sweetest cologne could not mask the stench of alcohol sweating through his pores. He was fun-loving and charming when sober, but when he got drunk on Fridays (payday), he spiraled into a dark recklessness and harrowing abuse. He was a Jekyll and Hyde man: a handsome countenance, a warm smile, and charisma that would light up any room; he was also a shameless womanizer with a temper and fists that would disrupt all the comforts of love and peace. He flirted with death by driving drunk and was charged with a few DUIs, oblivious to the hardships he caused the family. Every night I prayed for rain. Every day we drowned in his addiction.

The Confidante

However, in all the chaos, I knew he loved me. I was his secret confidante. We bonded during our Saturday nights when our family did odd jobs to make ends meet. While we swept and cleaned up the mall's huge parking lot in the darkness, he would share his innermost thoughts with me, including what his girlfriend was like. Even if it was highly inappropriate information for a child, it made me feel special. I loved being a daddy's girl, but the dirty little secrets felt like the greatest betrayal, inflicting a million little cuts on my mother's heart.

Eventually, our relationship changed, and we were no longer close. I longed for my father's presence—his infectious laughter, passion for music, zest for life, and even his forbidden stories of love and lust. It would be two decades before I would get him back in my life in a meaningful way.

The Fight

Being close to Dad made me the peacemaker in our household when World War III broke out. One night, the fight began as it often did—he came home drunk. The noise of the arguing woke me out of a deep sleep, but that night was different. The screaming was more urgent and higher pitched, and the moaning was deep and baritone, full of agony and desperation.

Even in his intoxication, I could always talk Dad down. So, I jumped out of bed and headed toward their bedroom. It was like running into the eye of the storm rather than away from it. I woke some of my siblings to help. We made our way down the dark hallway and pounded on the locked bedroom door. Our mother yelled to stay away ... to go back to sleep. The sounds of her screaming and Dad moaning kept us pounding our little fists, harder and harder, on the door until they hurt. But neither came to open the door.

Combining the force of our small feet, we kicked the door down. The old wooden door came crashing down with the molding still attached to the door, almost hitting them both. Then, we were the ones screaming. Dad straddled Mom with his hands wrapped around her neck. Mom was unrecognizable because her face was covered in blood.

Despite the blood on her face and Dad's hands on her neck, Mom began trying to calm us down. I remember her yelling at us saying, "Kids, calm down, calm down kids. The blood ... it's not me. It's your father's. Stop screaming. I'm OK. It's not me who's bleeding; it's your father."

In defending herself, Mom had picked up the heavy, black, rotary telephone and hit him over the head. Dad had a nasty gash on his forehead near his temple, and his blood was streaming down onto her face. He was motionless as she had a death grip on his testicles, which is why he was moaning so loudly. The fight was at an impasse until we broke the door down. Ironically, the one who was covered in blood was the one who was in control.

We finally calmed down. Then, Dad, still moaning, rolled off onto his side. Finally, they let one another go, but the trauma would remain for a long time.

The Escape Plan Celebration

That night my mother decided to file for divorce. They had been married 11 years, but the joy of marriage did not last long—he was an alcoholic, and he loved the ladies. Their relationship became argumentative, tumultuous, and full of peril. She initially vowed to stay in the marriage and see us through our private high school graduations because she didn't feel she could afford it on her own, working as a city clerk. But that night, she realized that she might not live to see us graduate, or she could end up in prison for killing Dad in self-defense. Then, her children would lose both parents.

So, she devised an escape plan: she went back to night school in secret and became a magistrate judge. My dad never knew because he often did not come home at night. On the day of her graduation, her friends threw a surprise graduation party to celebrate both her completion of the program and her official filing for divorce. We wore rainbow T-shirts, proclaiming "Here Come [no 's' for humor] the Judge." That was a day worth celebrating! My mom was appointed as a magistrate judge, and years later, she would be reappointed as a judge by then Governor of Delaware, Joe Biden.

Young children are not supposed to be happy when their parents get divorced, but life with Dad had not been easy for Mom—emotionally, physically or financially. Alcohol addiction caused him to spiral out of control with finances, infidelity, and violence. Although being without our dad left a tremendous void, I am so grateful that our mother did an amazing job raising us as a single mom.

A Fortuitous Proverbs Meeting

"He who finds a wife, finds a good thing."
Proverbs 18:22 (KJV)

After the divorce, Dad's life continued to spiral out of control. He had several near-death experiences driving under the influence, loss of relationships, and work demotions, and he didn't pay his taxes (Mom always did his household paperwork). He hit rock bottom. Until then, nothing—not two previous marriages, not success in corporate banking, not even his children—was enough to pull him out of the abyss of alcohol addiction. But fortuitously, Dad attended a banking conference in Florida, where he met a "remarkable woman who loved the Lord," as he described her. Finally, he wanted someone more than he wanted alcohol, partying, or other women; he wanted Bertha, a high-spirited, faith-filled woman from California.

Bertha was saved, and if he wanted to be a part of her life, she demanded he give up alcohol and come to know the Lord. After some soul searching, Dad found a church home in Philadelphia. However, Bertha told the pastor that she had seen him in his *element* and refused to marry a man who drank. Dad told me that one night he locked hands with Pastor Waters, and that was it. His sobriety lasted 20 years without one sip of alcohol since that day of steadfast and faith-filled prayer.

Lessons in Faith and Transformation of a Man

"Therefore, if any man be in Christ, he is a new creature: old things are passed away; behold all things become new."
2 Corinthians 5:17 (KJV)

Fast forward 20 years ... Dad became a faith-filled man of God. A fierce prayer warrior, he became the leader of the men's ministry and the marriage ministry and was active in the theater ministry in his church. He went to Bible college and became an ordained minister. He also became an entrepreneur in Our Global Vision/Next Level Leadership business. He was promoted to director and became a corporate trainer, and he led online trainings internationally. He recruited me, and he built a diverse team and distribution network throughout the world. He collaborated and built his own team in India. These connections and accomplishments were life-changing.

Then life took a turn for the worst. We were heartbroken to learn in 2014 that Dad had a rare cancer arising in the mediastinal part of his chest cavity that later metastasized to his liver, lungs, and bones. Here he was, in the midst of his greatest storm, and he was flourishing and thriving in ministry, leadership, and entrepreneurship. He vowed to fight it and remained positive throughout his course of treatments with chemotherapy and radiation. His faith in God and the strength of his marriage were seeing him through. During this time, he finished a book with Bertha, *Our Marriage, Our Redemption* and asked on his death bed that it be published.

As the cancer progressed, he met every day with grace. The end was difficult because the pain in his bones was excruciating. It was difficult to watch him struggle for air—gasping, gurgling, and drowning in his own secretions. The morphine masked the pain briefly, but it would come crashing back like monstrous tsunami waves, rushing in to devour his body. The pain never stopped him. Between gasps for air, he was still praising God before he died on May 27, 2015.

Through his example of faith and transformation, I learned, "If you declare with your mouth that Jesus is Lord, and believe in your heart that God raised him from the dead, you will be saved." (Romans 10:9, NLT). I learned that marriage is a covenant journey best traveled with God as your compass to find love, peace, joy, trust, and faithfulness. His marriage to Bertha was ordained, a match made from heaven, and I am grateful she was an instrument of the Lord that helped save him. Honoring his marriage to her was a chance for him to be in covenant with God and redeem his honor.

Dad wanted desperately for me, my siblings, and his grandchildren to learn about and come to know the Lord, utilizing the tools in our spiritual toolbox to break generational curses. Managing family, marriage and career can be a struggle, but the important thing is that my husband and I have been inspired to fight for our imperfect love with their example of faith, love, passion, and purpose. Most of all, I learned that by the time my dad took his final breath, I was in awe of God's power to transform a man, heal my wounds, make it rain, and bring him home.

Life is a constant reminder that all endings—good or bad—lead to new beginnings. We must find ways to be resilient through the trials and tribulations that we encounter along our own unique path. We can all find joy in our journey.

About Dr. Andrea

Photo credit: Jen Dworek

Growing up in the inner city and enrolling in college at the age of 14, Dr. Andrea Jeffress knows what it means to receive a hand up and not a handout. She is a Yale-trained, board-certified OB/GYN with an interest in advanced minimally invasive surgical techniques, such as hysteroscopy, laparoscopy, and robotic-assisted surgery.

As a physician entrepreneur, video marketer, and business connector, Dr. Andrea utilizes her vast network, wealth of knowledge, and unique experiences to motivate, guide, and connect others to build a plan for a brighter future. Beyond the walls of medicine, Dr. Andrea is on a journey to find joy in business, launching ventures such as DrJeffressMD, Smart Jocks, Blade Doctors, and Zenedge Energy Drinks. As a servant leader, she enjoys giving back as an advisory board member of the Kingdom International Economic Development Corporation, Mercyhurst University, and Erie Bank. She is an Athena Business Leadership Award winner and a member of Delta Sigma Theta Sorority, Inc.

Connect with Dr. Andrea

Let's be social and connect with me @drjeffressmd!

https://www.facebook.com/drjeffressmd

https://www.linkedin.com/in/drjeffressmd/

https://www.instagram.com/drjeffressmd/

https://twitter.com/drjeffressmd

Learn more on my website, https://drjeffressmd.com/.

Follow my journey to joy in business:

https://www.instagram.com/bladedoctorsllc/

https://www.facebook.com/bladedoctorsLLC/

https://twitter.com/bladedoctorsllc

https://www.facebook.com/Smartjocks

https://www.instagram.com/smart_jocks/

https://twitter.com/smart_jocks

https://www.instagram.com/zenedgeusa/

Perspective and Self-Care

Dr. Sarah L. Joint, BS, DC, NCRME

"I know my worth, I've paid dearly for every ounce of it."[6]

~ Alfa Holden

In 2018, I became pregnant with twins from a round of fertility treatments and suddenly found myself in the middle of a very traumatic divorce. I gave birth after very serious complications for both myself and my twins. They were in the neonatal intensive care unit (NICU) for six weeks, and I was hospitalized for two weeks.

Perspective

A few weeks after giving birth, I sat down next to a woman at a restaurant. We began talking, and she had a story similar to mine, except her story forced her and her kids to move back in with her parents. She was struggling, but she was super excited because she just got a great job and felt sure this was the break she needed for her and her kids. I inquired what the job was, and honestly, I can't remember, only that she was so excited it paid $11 an hour! I thought to myself, *Wow, how can that be life changing? How can you support kids on that?* I smiled and said, "That's great. I'm so happy for you." At that moment, I realized there's a lot to be said about perspective. She was happy and going to make it work on

---

[6] Alfa Holden,
https://www.goodreads.com/quotes/search?utf8=%E2%9C%93&q=%22I+know+my+worth%2C+I%E2%80%99ve+paid+dearly+for+every+ounce+of+it.%E2%80%9D&commit=Search

far less than I had. I was extremely grateful for both my education and career and realized I shouldn't feel so sorry for myself.

I struggled through the first year being a single twin-mom, while running my business and taking them to work with me for the first six months. I'm eternally grateful for my friends and coworkers that helped me daily through this time.

Then, while barely holding my life together, the unimaginable happened. Daddy died. *He died!* This is a blow no one wants, but why did it have to happen right at this moment in my life? I had experienced so much trauma lately. I was just trying to get through, and the person who was always there for me, no matter what, just died. Let me tell you, there is no amount of therapy, self-love, or time that can change this moment in my life. The day his heart stopped beating, a part of me died. On really bad days, I remind myself that Daddy always made it clear what he wanted for me: to be happy, self-sufficient, and always able to figure things out if he ever wasn't around. You know what? I am! And I am killing it because he raised a fiercely persistent, smart, hard-working woman. (*RIP Daddy, forever connected at the heart, August 9, 2019)*

"Death changes everything. Time changes nothing. I still miss the sound of your voice, the wisdom in your advice, the stories of your life and just being in your presence. So no, time changes nothing. I miss you just as much today as I did the day you died. I just miss you."[7]

~ Unknown

The next few weeks after Daddy died, I functioned in a haze. It was indescribable. I talked to my therapist, drank too much, and cried multiple times a day. Then I found something worse than

---

[7] Death Changes Everything, Time Changes Nothing - Live Life Happy, https://livelifehappy.com/life-quotes/death-changes-everything-time-changes-nothing/

my grief over losing my father: dealing with my almost seven-year-old's grief. My dad lived right next to us and frequently took my son fishing, for rides on the tractor, or just spent time with him. How do you explain grief to a seven-year-old while grieving yourself? It's agonizingly hard.

A few days after my dad passed, my grandmother died. My poor mom had to bury her husband and mom the same week. I felt absolutely terrible for her. *Perspective:* even though my life was difficult at this time it could always be worse.

Six months after Daddy died, my 14-year-old lab, Drake, died. He was one of a kind. Labs are notorious chewers, yet he never chewed. He didn't leave the yard but was never trained to stay in it. He was scared of thunder storms and loved baked goods. No cage could contain him. The vet said he had tumors on his liver and one had burst, a common condition in older labs. They said surgery was an option but more than likely they wouldn't be able to control the bleeding, and he would die during surgery. Surgery was thousands of dollars, but at this point in my life, I would have done anything to keep him from dying. I never got to make that choice. Drake made it for me, passing away before surgery could even be scheduled.

Self-Care

I was at my breaking point and realized I couldn't pour from an empty cup. I had to do something, or I really was going to lose it. I was still seeing my therapist regularly, but I knew I needed more. I started to make it a point to regularly get a chiropractic adjustment. It seems dumb that a chiropractor was not making time for something I preach to my patients to do, but I wasn't doing it. Then, I started getting monthly massages. This was all well and good but so much of my life was on such a tight schedule. I never had any free time.

Even when I wasn't working and my kids were with their dad, I was stuck in this mindset of always having to do something: to get the laundry done, or go to work and finish things up, and on and on. I started to set aside time weekly when I purposely made no plans. If I wanted to sleep in, I did. If I slept in, wanted to move to the couch, and never put my bra on, I did. If I felt like getting something done at work would make me feel better, I would go to work and do it. If I felt like calling a friend and going out, I did. It was life changing. Just to tell myself I was worth investing in, that even though I have tons of responsibilities, it was OK to focus on myself even if only for a few hours.

Between being a single mom of three kids, losing Daddy (my rock), providing in every way for my children, being a homeowner with few home-repair-skills, being a doctor who patients depended on, and a business owner responsible for employees, all made me feel like I had to be everyone's everything. It was exhausting, and sometimes still is, but taking time to care for myself has greatly decreased that anxiety.

Eventually, after my divorce, I felt healed enough to start dating. As usual, my timing was impeccable, and weeks after I started online dating, the pandemic hit and everything closed down. Where do you go on a first date during a pandemic? My first date was with a kind soul in a gas station parking lot. We grabbed smoothies and sat on the curb. He swore he had more class than this. We laughed. We went on over a dozen dates. He was so kind; then he ghosted me. I was in shock, and this set the tone for the next few years of horrific dating disasters. I'm not sure if I was unlucky, or just had an unrealistic set of qualities I was looking for, but it was crazy how hard this online dating thing was from the military men on some far away top-secret mission who suddenly needed high-dollar gift cards to men who I'm fairly positive were serial killers and going to chop me up and bury me in the basement. It was unbelievable. I was asked to go on a drug deal in the middle of one date. On another date, the man announced after we ordered our drinks that he wasn't going to pay for mine if I didn't have sex with him after the date. I put money down on the table to pay for both of our drinks and left before our order arrived.

It was at this point that I decided to document my dating disasters, mainly for self-therapy, but I found it so entertaining I could actually envision it as a bestseller. As I started keeping notes, online dating morphed into more than finding a suitable mate and into something more like a research project for my book. Toward the end, I would go on a date and instead of thinking this could be the one, I just wondered what crazy story he could add to the book.

Then, on one night in early January, I walked into an Applebee's, and the final chapter of my book began. He is attentive, thoughtful, great with my kids, helpful around the house, and beyond supportive of me and our goals. I finally found my unicorn.

Throughout it all, the number one thing I learned is to listen to myself. It took me a long time, but I have developed the ability to intuitively know what I need, like taking a couple hours to myself every week for unscheduled time. Sometimes the thoughts are half-baked but eventually come into focus. For example, a few months ago, I was really struggling at work. I was stressed and wanted some things to happen, but they just weren't. I knew it wasn't the Universe, it was me. I was the problem. But how do I fix that? I eventually decided to do a reiki session and dusted off the vision board I had made a year prior. I added some things to the board (life changes and so does your vision) and put it up on my dresser, so I am able to look at each word and image as I put on my jewelry every morning. I don't know which part helped or how it helped, but I can tell you it worked. *Listen to yourself.*

About Dr. Sarah

Dr. Sarah L. Joint is a chiropractor practicing in Erie, Pa. She is the founder of Joint Chiropractic, as well as a nationally registered certified medical examiner which allows her to perform DOT/CDL physicals.

While Dr. Joint did not previously aspire to be an author, this opportunity presented itself at the perfect time. Not only is she able to share her traumatic experiences and how she persevered, but also use the opportunity as a stepping stone to her upcoming book. She hopes to provide readers with comedic relief by telling her crazy online dating adventures.

Connect with Dr. Sarah

https://www.JointChiropracticErie.com

https://www.DOTPhysicalsErie.com

Conquering the Boulders in My Path

Christal Lepak

"It's easy enough to pray when you're in distress but continuing to pray even when your crisis has passed is like a sealing process, helping your soul hold tight to its good attainment."

~ Elizabeth Gilbert[8]

Wow! I thought my life was going to be different. I remember when I was in high school, how I'd spend my classes daydreaming, each fantasy taking me to faraway places, especially Paris! Growing up, I saw how my mother struggled raising us kids alone and how she lived month to month on social security checks. A widow in the 70s with two kids—it was not easy for her, (or any woman during that time), but she sacrificed and struggled through. I thought, *No sir, that will not be me!* I was going to do something with my life, something *grand*. Maybe travel the world ... Paris first, of course! It seemed ideal since I had ancestral roots in France. I'd dream about walking along the Seine River to find a café, smell the pastries baking, hear the sounds of music playing from local street musicians, and see the painters selling their latest creations. I had it all planned out. I would have meals, sip wine, read books by the Eiffel Tower, see the great art works in The Louvre, and stroll the most famous avenue in Paris—the Champs-Élysées! With my eyes closed, I am whisked away to an alternate reality ... ahhh, Paris.

"Mom!"

---

[8] Gilbert, Elizabeth. 2006. *Eat, Pray, Love*. New York, NY: Viking Press.

Wait ... where was I? As my eyes opened, I was shaken back into reality and quickly reminded that this was certainly *not* Paris. No, this was my reality: the chaos of grocery shopping with my four children. "Mom! Did you hear me?" *No, dear child,* I thought, staring blankly back at her. I could not hear her; I was in my own world, yet again. However, it was no world I knew at present, or that I would ever know, it seemed. I was so tired of only having a few hours of sleep ... again. I was tired of being tired.

Here I was in my early 20s, with four children, standing in the grocery line trying to figure out how I got here. *No, girl,* I told myself. *You can't think like that. Come on, shake it off. Look how beautiful your children are.* As I looked over, two of my kids were smacking each other over something on the shelf in the aisle. Of course, it is placed at eye-level, making them want it even more (like most children) ... and me not having *more*. I broke up the fight and told myself to breathe; it would be OK. But that was just it, I was *not* OK. I thought about it every day—about being tired and stuck. I shook my head to snap out of it.

I looked over the contents of the cart and said a silent prayer, *Oh God, please let me have enough to make it through this month.* It seemed like this was our regular monthly conversation in which I plead, *Let's barter, God.* I made the meal plan and figured portions out down to the pound. Let's see, $80 for the six of us, this was a good month. Usually, we barely scraped $50 together. *He* (my now ex) would not allow me to get food-stamps. I wished we had them. Medical insurance, no; that was government run too. Can't have the government in our business.

The baby was nursing, so we didn't need formula, but times got tougher, and we had to use WIC (women, infants, and children government program), which provided milk and food to supplement. The garden's starting to produce, and grain is going down in price so I could grab that to grind for bread. Canning season was almost upon us, and I was grateful for that. It would be a hearty haul this year. When I scanned the protein options for the children, I saw five pounds of burger meat and a couple of whole chickens, but there wasn't enough in the budget. I looked at the kids, once again arguing and fighting in this congested line, and I hurried to pay for the groceries. We were over, of course, and I had to put back a few items, but I knew I could find substitutes for them in recipes.

Everyone was staring at me and the kids were so loud. I screamed inside, *Shove that shit down, girl! No one will care. You have responsibilities, and no one's here to help you. Just ... ahhh!* I shoved it all down.

Yeah, this is definitely *not* what I had in mind, but sometimes our choices lead us to paths we would not have consciously chosen. I still would have settled down, gotten married, and had children, just not this early in my life. After all, I was going to travel the world ... Paris, here I come! Reality sinks in, *Sorry, Chica, not today.* The grandiose dreams and plans I had were just that, dreams to make it out of a living hell where I didn't get to make any of my own choices. Reality grabbed hold and pulled me under—drowning me, stealing my breath, my life—was this it? Was this all there was? *God, get me out of this store.* I hung my head and quickly exited the store, frantically scanning for the van.

On my way home, as the children were occupied, listening to their music, I started letting my thoughts wander, *Why did I feel stuck?* Oh, yes, a bad marriage choice. I was young and naïve, but those grandiose dreams kept coming back to haunt me. One in particular—you know the one—the knight in shining armor who comes to whisk me away to Europe, Asia, and all over the world; someone to take me away from it all, from the pain of my reality. I felt like it was all a lie, and I paid for it dearly: for 11 and a half years I paid for it. I bought into the fairytale because I wanted it so badly. Now, I'm just trying to get home, get the groceries unloaded, and get dinner ready before *he* gets home. I said another prayer, *Lord, get me through this night. Please God, I'm so tired.*

After I got home, I put the kids to bed, took care of the house, took care of *him* (the husband), and in bed I silently prayed, again, *God, I know this is not the plan. Help me, please!* That night I had a dream. It went a little like this:

I was walking along a path, and at first, I was trying to figure out where I was and how I got there when I noticed a very bright light up ahead. It was quite a bit away and looked a little twisted, but it was lit up, and the light at the end beamed bright, so I decided to walk toward it. The strange part was, as I walked along the path, I noticed everything around me was dark—like you can't see your hand out in front of you dark. Wow! Scary.

I continued walking, and an overwhelming sense came over me that I knew I just needed to stay on the path, and I'd be safe. I started thinking of all the trials and tribulations I had growing up without a dad and with a single mom who had mental health trauma. I did not understand anything other than what I was told and taught from the elders in our family. Right about then, Thud*! What the heck? I look up and it was a huge boulder. How the heck am I going to get over this thing? Wait, where's that bright light I saw before?*

I studied the boulder. It was humongous! Maybe I could go around it and find a short cut? I don't know; it's awfully dark off the path. I looked up and thought that there was no way I could climb this. So, I decided to step off the path and go into the dark to find an easier way around this thing. Immediately, I was engulfed by a dark heaviness, as I tried to feel my way around. I could find nothing but more darkness, and then I started thinking I was never going to get through this thick dark. I needed to get back to the path. But how? I could not see anything! Panic hit me, Oh no! I'm lost! *Fumbling around I decided to retrace any familiar steps and finally made it back to where I started. Wow! That was way too scary.*

Continuing to look at the boulder in my way, I decided I would have to climb it. At first, I got a leg, a foot, an arm, and a hand up on it. "OK, girl," I said to myself out loud, "You got this!" and I climbed. But just as I thought the end was in sight, and I could make this climb, I lost my footing and fell to the ground. Thud! Ouch! WTH? Well, that went well, *I thought. Look, now I have cuts, bruises, and my butt hurts. As I sat there thinking—trying to figure out this puzzle—it just seemed the pieces were not going to fit. So, I sat there and cried. What else could I do? This all seemed so hopeless. How many bruises did I have to get? How many times did I have to fall down? Each time I'd fall, I'd get back up and climb a little bit higher up that boulder. But this last time I fell, it really hurt. I started doubting my own survival because the boulder was jagged in places and would cut me with every step I took. Some spots would seem OK, and then another section cut deep, and on and on it went. But this last climb nearly killed me from falling so far. Staring at this problem, this boulder, I decided enough was enough.*

I got up, dusted myself off, and cleaned up my wounds. Praying, for what seemed like the millionth time, I screamed, "Why? No way! Not this time! I'm not letting you win!" I said to this monstrosity, and, I started to climb. I climbed like I never did before, as if my whole life depended on it. Climb, girl, climb!" *I heard this voice ... where was it coming from? I saw some kind of support, and I stepped on it. I kept looking up, toward the top this time.* No, don't look down. You'll fall again. Remember, that was what you were doing when you fell the times before. Keep looking up, keep going ... *but I felt so weak. I'd been doing this forever, it seemed.* Just a little more, girl. *The cuts were burning, the bruises were hurting, my hands were numb from grabbing and pulling, but I kept climbing ... praying ... focusing ... letting go of everything else and allowing my gaze to lock in to the top of the boulder: one more leg, one more foot, one more arm, one more hand.* That's it, pull yourself up. You got it girl. Look!

Did I just make it? Did I just climb that? Look, the light! The Path! I knew it was not going to be smooth going down this boulder, but I knew as long as I kept my eye on the light—the finish line—I would make it back down the other side. It did not mean that I wasn't going to experience any more boulders along my path, but I knew now how I could get over and defeat them. Gathering years of strength and support from my faith, my personal accomplishments, and the many supportive women in my life, I knew I had this. As I started down the boulder, I said to myself, Come on girl, you got this! *I recounted the voices I heard telling me to keep going throughout the climb, and I heard,* Make each day count by being the best version of you that you can be. Seize every opportunity to improve and evolve. Everything else is temporary.

And now the real-life journey begins ...

About Christal

Christal Lepak is a proud mother of five children and two grandchildren. Tragically, she lost two daughters to the drug epidemic and to alcohol abuse. Throughout the *boulders* of her life, she achieved a bachelor's degree in history/government and a master's degree in education. She has been teaching children, youth, and adults in northwestern Pennsylvania for over a decade. Through her experiences of love and loss, she shares her deeply personal testimony of strength, courage, patience, perseverance, and confidence to rise above life's trials and tribulations. Christal spends her time advocating for change and equality for all. She loves teaching adults and helping them get back on their feet and is busy doing local outreach work with underserved youth communities.

Connect with Christal

Instagram: https://www.instagram.com/clepak3/

TikTok: https://www.tiktok.com/@christallepak

Facebook:
https://www.facebook.com/profile.php?id=100079918293733

Email: clepak2657@gmail.com

I Remember

Cathi Gg Mitchell

"Be the person you needed when you were younger."[9]

~ Ayesha Siddiqi

Up until my 40s, I was unable to remember many positive memories about my childhood. Though I knew they were there, I had difficulty recalling them. But there are most certainly some things that I will never forget. For starters, I will never forget lying on my bed sobbing as a child. My little dog, Fluffy, jumped up onto the bed. Sensing my sadness, she somehow forced her way through my tightly guarded arms to nestle beside me. The feeling that ensued from the encounter led to a self-proclaimed lifelong promise: from that day forward, I vowed to make someone smile for every tear I cried. Little did I know what an incredible feat that would be.

It wasn't until I went to my first sleepover that I started to think I was different. I will never forget the feeling of waiting for my friend's dad to crawl into bed with us; nor the feeling of thinking something was wrong with me because he didn't. Those formative years were full of a lot of confusion, and so many secrets to keep. I had terrifying things happening to me (and witnessed them happening to others) with no one to tell. So, I told all my secrets to Fluffy. She would just listen and snuggle.

---

[9] Ayesha Siddiqi, quoted in https://voicesforcasachildren.org/casa-help-guides/be-the-person-you-needed-when-you-were-younger/

I don't remember when my dad moved out, but I had to start going to his apartment to visit him. I know that I never felt safe there. I will never forget the day a man walked into his apartment while he was downstairs in the bar. I was still in bed. I pretended to be sleeping as the man crawled into bed with me. I cried and prayed that my dad would come to save me. When he left and I went looking for my dad, I found him drinking a beer with the man and exchanging cash.

What's wrong with me? I don't remember when I started asking myself this question, but I asked it often and for different reasons. I didn't feel like I acted or responded like others. I'll never forget watching my mom cook and having a hot spoon land on my foot and how the physical pain made me forget about my emotional pain. This led to years of self-harm with heated metal spoons. The alcohol that was used to make me more cooperative also helped numb the physical pain and quiet my head. It became another negative coping skill.

I loved to color. I'd give the pages to people as gifts and cherished their smiles. I always loved making people laugh and often got notes sent home about being the class clown. We didn't have much money, but I would often find things around the house to make gifts for my friends and teachers at school. I wish I could say that school was a place where I felt safe, but that was not the case. The clutter in my mind started to be reflected in my surroundings, and my desk and cubby at school became a mess. My teachers didn't recognize that or any other signs of my trauma. In fact, they actually added to it. For instance, in sixth grade, my teacher emptied out my cubby onto the floor in front of the class and announced loudly that I was a dirty, dirty girl, while some of my classmates laughed. I sat on the floor crying as I cleaned my things up, wishing that Fluffy was there to comfort me.

My feelings of not being safe only escalated when my brother found my journals and shared them with my mom. Every secret was finally out. I was full of so many emotions. My mom asked why I hadn't told her about everything before, but nothing changed. I started keeping things inside. This took its toll when both school and home were overwhelming, and I had no outlet for my emotions. I couldn't handle it anymore and had very mixed feelings when I woke up after overdosing on my mom's medication.

Attending a youth group in junior high, I heard that Jesus loved me just as I was and that he wanted to spend time with me. The way I had been feeling, that seemed too good to be true. But, I thought, What do I have to lose? What I discovered, is that it was my lack of hope, although two more suicide attempts would ensue before I began to experience true healing and joy.

I ended up moving in with my youth group leaders, Max and Lesley Andrzejewski. I will never forget the first night that I stayed over. Habitually, I waited for my foster dad to come and get in bed with me. The fact that Max never did, along with the love and care they continually showed me, was confusing at first. It was hard to trust anyone, and I was quite certain that as soon as I did something wrong, they would want to send me away.

But that never happened. I was starting to better understand that unconditional love I had heard Jesus had for me. My foster parents, and foster brothers and sisters, continue to be a source of joy.

In my psychology and social work classes in college, I learned so much about myself. I began to learn answers to my perpetual question, *What's wrong with me?* and tools to better address it. I learned that becoming a Christian didn't end this battle for me; however, it sure helped me feel like I wasn't fighting it alone anymore! College, and a Christian fellowship I took part in there, strengthened my faith and gave me a strong desire to help others on their healing journey. I really had a heart to work with children because I didn't want any of them to hurt like I did as a child.

After college graduation, I worked several jobs in the social services field helping children and coached eight different sports.

I went on to create and direct a multitude of programs for children, teens, and those with special needs. I did a lot of advocacy work and volunteered thousands of hours. I wanted to be anywhere children were, helping them create happy memories, build character, find hope, provide a listening ear, give them a voice, and help them find joy.

I have had several different therapists throughout the years, and they have all helped in different ways. But when my health started to fail me and really started to affect my job as a therapist, I started to see another therapist myself. I sought one through our employee assistance program. The sessions began addressing my declining health and its impact on my life and job. But the wellspring of joy flowed from there, and my wonderful therapist, Michelle Domowicz, MA, helped me to thoroughly connect the trauma from my childhood to my difficulty with relationships, addiction issues, physical health, and more. She helped finally answer my perpetual question, *What's wrong with me?* It was a very long journey but well worth it. She used many different effective therapy modalities throughout the years, but the most effective was eye movement desensitization and reprocessing (EMDR). EMDR is an evidenced based therapeutic approach to treating trauma and post-traumatic stress disorder (PTSD). The EMDR sessions helped me live with some of the traumatic memories I had been battling. They kept creeping out and seeping onto others because I couldn't handle them by myself.

My youngest brother, my sister, and I were always close. I didn't see much of my other siblings. My mom had moved to Georgia with my sister, and while she was alive, I failed to see all of her efforts to connect with me. Before she passed away from complications removing a brain tumor, she made all of us promise that we would stay close. This led to an annual sibling reunion every Fourth of July weekend. We all take turns hosting it, and I look forward to it every year. It fills me to overflowing with joy.

My mom passed away a few days before Thanksgiving, so I go to Georgia every Thanksgiving to have a memorial celebration of her life. We practice childhood traditions and established several new ones. We also go and visit my mom's grave together. Every Christmas, I go to my brother's house in Delaware to celebrate with his family. I try and get there on other holidays as well. Every visit, I remember more and more about my childhood.

When COVID-19 hit and none of us were able to travel, I initiated weekly video calls. We continue to meet every Sunday night at eight o'clock. This is always the highlight of my week and has been a great source of healing as we discuss childhood memories often. It has helped me to remember good parts of my childhood otherwise forgotten, to learn even more about my mom, and grow closer to my siblings.

I did an ancestry test a few years ago which uncovered a lot about my mom's childhood. I participated in a generational Zoom call for a while and got to know a lot more of my extended family. Knowing about my mom's childhood has helped me understand some of her deficits as a parent and my perception of her love for me. I wish I would have known these things when she was still alive. The knowledge would have definitely changed our relationship. However, since I can't do that now, I've let it motivate me to better my relationship with my daughters.

God has blessed me with two amazing adult daughters. I know that I allowed my childhood trauma to affect a great deal of my parenting. Having conversations with them about my childhood, taking accountability, validating their feelings, and having the memories be more manageable has really improved our relationships.

There may always be things from my childhood that I won't be able to forget, but what brings me immeasurable joy is remembering that I am loved by God and my family!

About Cathi

Cathi Gg (Godgirl) Mitchell has been fascinated with words as long as she can remember. She has been a contributing writer for a multitude of newsletters, magazines, and newspapers. Her favorite is the Christian Community Herald. Gg is also a published poet and is currently in the process of writing her first poetry book. After overcoming a traumatic childhood, Gg became the first person in her family to graduate college. She is certified in ecosystemic structural family therapy and has won numerous awards. These include the Women Making History and the National Alliance of Mental Illness Service Recognition Awards. Yet, she feels her greatest accomplishment is being the mom of two enlightened, intelligent, and remarkable adult daughters.

Connect with Cathi

Email: wordshurtwordsheal@gmail.com

Facebook: https://www.facebook.com/cathi.mitchell

Instagram: https://www.instagram.com/cathiggmitchell/

The Darkest Storms Bring Rainbows

Tharifa Noor

"Happiness is not a destination. It's a journey."

~ Anonymous

In the depths of despair, when darkness threatened to consume every ounce of hope, I made a choice—a choice to reclaim my life, to rise above the ashes of my past, and to embrace a future filled with joy and abundance. This chapter is not just my story; it's a testament to the power of redemption and the indomitable spirit within each of us.

The abuse I endured from a boyfriend, both physically and mentally, was part of a pattern. Feeling unworthy and settling for less than what I deserved was familiar to me. It stemmed from my childhood and carried over into my adult life.

I first married in my early 20s. At the time, I was a flight attendant with Singapore Airlines, living in Singapore. I met my husband on a blind date. He was 11 years older than I was. When we got married, I became a stepmom with three young boys. He was a great husband and father to his children. He was a very successful businessman who owned an oil company and was making millions. We traveled often and lived a very luxurious lifestyle.

We were married for six years before the marriage started to crumble due to his infidelity. He promised me that he would never cheat on me again, but that didn't last! I had to walk away from that marriage. It seemed I was repeating history because that was my environment growing up.

My second marriage lasted for 15 years. The abuse I endured in that marriage was more subtle. He was an online gambling and trading addict. That relationship ended in betrayal ... again.

After my second divorce, I met my boyfriend. I thought I had found my soulmate and the perfect relationship. We lived a life of luxury, jet-setting around the world, and dining in the finest restaurants. However, behind the glamorous facade, a dark cloud loomed. His drinking and controlling behaviors emerged, turning my fairytale into a nightmare. Day by day, his drinking increased, and his moods became unpredictable, jealous, and questioning. The charming and caring partner I once knew transformed from Dr. Jekyll to Mr. Hyde, inflicting verbal, mental, and physical abuse upon me. I became paralyzed with fear, constantly walking on eggshells and losing sight of my own identity.

Why did I stay in that relationship? Why didn't I just leave? These questions haunted me as I struggled to find the strength to break free. I believed there was a good side to him, a glimmer of hope that things would change. I tried to nurture and understand him, thinking I could help him overcome his demons. But in doing so, I allowed him to take control of my life, eroding my self-worth with each passing day.

Some days, I felt paralyzed from the physical and mental torture. The name calling, the cheating accusations, and the constant control of my every move were killing me bit by bit. I began to struggle getting out of bed and going to work. My body was in so much pain; I was emotionally drained.

During this time, I owned a hair salon and spa. It was my dream business. I was putting my heart, soul, and money into this venture. My goal was to help women look and feel good. My salon and spa provided various services such as spray tanning, eyelash extensions, and hair, makeup, and nail services. My business was thriving in the beginning; however, my health was declining. The juxtaposition was ironic.

There were days I had to cover bruises on my face. I endured many nights of physical abuse from him when he got home from a night of drinking. Often, he would show up at my salon and check on me to see if I was helping any male clients at work. His jealousy and insecurity, although unprovoked by me, ruled my life.

I was very good at pretending everything was OK on the outside. I was walking around wearing a mask. On the inside, I felt shame, sadness, and loneliness. My business was going well, but I was a walking time bomb.

Looking back, I had all the signs that I was not in control of my situation and environment, but I was too afraid to ask for help. I thought I could help him with his drinking and craziness by bowing down to his needs and his roller coaster behaviors. I was living to please him and not living for my own happiness.

Everything changed when I slept in the car on a cold night in October, after recovering from my boyfriend breaking my jaw. This was my defining moment. The worst thoughts came to my mind, and I knew I had to do something drastic. I called an abuse hotline but hung up when a woman answered. I started crying, praying, and asking God, *Why me? I can't do this anymore.* Then I heard a voice say, "It's not you!"

I felt like lightning struck me. I sat up, wiped my tears, and yelled, "It's not me; it's him!" I felt adrenaline rushing through me. I made a decision. I was going to live my life; I didn't need him.

I recalled my life before him—it was fulfilling and wonderful. After my second divorce, I had a great career as a fashion stylist, my own apartment ... and *freedom!* I traveled all over the world, and no one told me what to do, how to act, what to wear, when to speak, or when not to speak.

In that moment, my true desire to live and not be trapped in an isolated nightmare became crystal clear. The flickering light within me ignited, and I made a life-altering decision to control my destiny. With every ounce of courage, I left my abusive boyfriend, choosing to prioritize my well-being and safety over everything else. It was a pivotal moment of acceptance and release. I let go.

As I gathered the shattered pieces of my life, I embarked on a journey of healing and self-discovery. I immersed myself in accepting what had happened, acknowledging the pain and trauma I had endured. It was a difficult path, but with each step, I reclaimed my power and refused to be defined by my past.

The next phase of my journey involved releasing with love. I recognized that holding onto anger, resentment, and bitterness only kept me shackled to the pain. So, I chose to release those negative emotions, not just for him, but for myself. It was a profound act of self-love, a declaration that I deserved happiness and freedom from my past.

I never would have imagined that my life could be this amazing, filled with joy and abundance. I wake up every day feeling excited about what's to come, and ready to face the challenges and opportunities that God has in store for me. The days of living in doubt, fear, and limiting beliefs are over. The days of being afraid to take chances, make decisions, or believe that I wasn't good enough to be successful are over. I have turned my pain into power.

Today, I am living my best life at 64. Since moving from my 13-year home in Hawaii to the East Coast, I have embarked on a new path. I embraced living in a harmonious state of being. I have invested in myself by studying the Ayurvedic lifestyle with self-healing techniques such as implementing meditation, yoga practices, using herbs and spices, making natural remedies, and learning the chakras. I studied the psychology of the mind through Matrix Success International, and it has the biggest impact on how I think and operate. I also studied Chi Nei Tsang, a holistic healing practice for the gut.

I have a network marketing business that provides products from several brands. Our marketplace connects you directly with the best products, ensuring you find exactly what you need from the health and wellness arena to many other areas of service. I am an Amazon bestselling author in the anthology, *20 Lives Ignited: How 20 Women Over 60 are Creating Success on Their Own Terms.* I raised $15,000 for the Wounded Warrior Project when I participated in the Ms. Health and Fitness Competition. I work with JP Events, doing charity fundraising to help children's hospitals. I am a lifestyle coach helping clients overcome anxiety and fear, bringing balance to their lives by working with the mind, body, and spirit. I help clients by customizing programs to their specific needs, using 1-to-1 and small group coaching. I am your go-to lady if you are living with anxiety, fear, procrastination, limiting beliefs, self-doubt, and/or despair.

I now recognize my purpose in life. I love life, and I love what I do. It is my mission to help others do the same! Joy and abundance are a way of life, and I am now living it.

About Tharifa

Tharifa Noor was a mother, wife, and grandmother living in Mifflinburg, Pa., at the time of writing this chapter. She began her career as a flight attendant, traveling the world. Tharifa's career expanded to fashion stylist for Canadian celebrities and entrepreneurs. She also worked in a modeling agency, helping women with grooming and personal deportment.

Tharifa always had a passion for health and fitness. Her fitness goals followed her into her 50s, as she was a fitness competitor in the 2017 Hawaii National Physical Competition. She also participated in the Ms. Health and Fitness Competition and raised $15,000 for the Wounded Warrior Project.

She experienced crippling anxiety throughout her life. Being a lifelong health and wellness advocate, she decided to address her health struggles by utilizing holistic medicine. She studied Chi Nei Tsang and an Ayurvedic lifestyle, which helps bring people's minds, bodies, and spirits into balance.

Tharifa studied the Thinking Into Results (TIR) Program from the Proctor Gallagher Institute. This program teaches about mindset and how it affects wellbeing. She practiced and applied the skills she studied while actively participating in a weekly mastermind with other spiritual healers and her own wealth mindset community, Matrix Success Network.

Having gained an enormous amount of skill and experience during her personal transformation, Tharifa helped many of her clients reclaim their goals with regard to health, wellness, fitness, relationships, and career paths, becoming a better version of themselves. She helped others transform through their personal journeys.

Tharifa also had a shopping network where she guided her clients in the use of natural products for their daily lives.

It is with profound sadness that we celebrate the life of our sister, our loving, caring, and amazing Tharifa, who passed away on July 30, 2023. We are devastated by the loss of this beautiful soul. Her legacy will live on forever through the books, and she will continue to help so many women.

Aloha, Tharifa ...

We pray for family and friends.

Connect with Tharifa's Work

Shopping Network: https://mydailychoice.com/healingelement

Website: http://www.babetteryou.com

Facebook: https://www.facebook.com/tharifa

If you or anyone you know is dealing with domestic violence, don't hesitate to get help. Call one of the numbers below. The women of *We Choose Joy* want you to live your best life, safely.

National Domestic Violence Hotline

1-800-799-7233

SafeNet, Erie PA

814-454-8161

A Complete STOP

Remlee Peck

"You can't wait until life isn't hard anymore before you decide to be happy."[10]

~ Jane Marczewski (aka Nightbirde)

Just like that ... my life changed. Oh, I had fallen before, haven't we all? But this time was different. This time shook me to the core.

It was always my nature to squeeze as much as possible into every waking moment. So that fateful night, not only was I unloading groceries, I was also planting the flowers that I just bought. As I finished watering them, I noticed my American flag had gotten twisted around the pole above my porch. Without hesitation, I took a few steps and jumped up from where I was, planning to grab the bottom of the flag and straighten it. I never thought about getting the ladder first—big mistake! It was then that it happened, and I came crashing down onto my concrete driveway.

I'm not sure how long I lay there before I looked at my watch. Maybe I hit my head against the porch or was in shock, because it took a few minutes for reality to set in. I was surprised to discover that it was after 11 p.m. I struggled to get up, but my left leg kept buckling underneath me. I couldn't stand, no matter how hard I tried. I said to myself, *Oh, no. What have you done now, Rem*? Tears welled up inside, and I was scared. Right then and there, it

---

[10] Marczewski, Jane "Nightbirde," *America's Got Talent* 2021 Audition.

hit me: my life as I knew it had come to an abrupt halt ... *a complete STOP.*

I began to wonder who would even see me lying on the driveway at that hour. I didn't have my cell phone because I had left it on the kitchen counter with all the groceries. Looking around, I saw no one. My heart sank. Just as I was about to desperately call out for help, I heard the sound of footsteps coming toward me. I looked up to see who it was, but the face was shadowed by the streetlight. I heard him ask, "Are you OK?" I didn't recognize his voice, but I was relieved that someone was coming to my rescue. From out of nowhere, he appeared like an angel to me at that moment, my knight in shining armor, a gift from God. I asked him what his name was, and all he said was, "Michael."

Michael gently picked me up and carried me into the house. It was as if I was weightless. He carefully put me down in a kitchen chair and handed my cell phone to me. I called 911. I had never seen Michael before that night; fortunately for me, he was in the right place at the right time. Michael finished putting away my groceries before the ambulance arrived. I couldn't thank him enough for helping me. I never saw Michael again after that night. I didn't get his last name and no one in my neighborhood knew who he was.

The orthopedic doctor was very concerned when he looked at my X-rays. "Bottom line," he said, "you have two choices: either be non-weight-bearing for the next 90 days so your fracture can heal on its own or undergo surgery and hope for the best outcome." I chose the 90-day option. I figured 90 days—that's just 12 weeks—only three months without standing on that leg. I can do that; I have to do that. It certainly wasn't what I had originally planned to do over the summer, but I had made my choice and was determined to walk again, in even less time than that.

The first two weeks of June were spent in the hospital, making sure the swelling in my leg was being monitored and no blood clots had formed. For the remainder of the month, I resided in a rehab facility while friends equipped my home and prepared a wheelchair ramp for me.

I dealt with many emotions that first month, mostly annoyance with my carelessness and the painful situation I had put myself in. Then came a great sadness for the loss of my day-to-day freedom. I was becoming my own worst enemy with my negative self-talk, and I recognized it. I knew I couldn't change what had happened, but I also acknowledged that I desperately needed to amend the way I was thinking and talking to myself about it because neither one was doing me any good. I needed a complete reset ... emphasis on the word, "I." I didn't realize it then, but this was becoming a defining moment in my life.

I lost my independence that summer. I spent June, July, and August in a leg brace and a wheelchair. I had to accept being dependent upon others for the first time in my adult life. I wasn't able to drive, do laundry, or mow my lawn. It was a humbling experience. I didn't want to be a burden to my family or friends. So, I made the decision to call that wheelchair my *chariot* because it was the *vehicle* I used to help me stay strong and carry on in my home, like a gladiator fighting the battle of his life. This was becoming my personal battle: first to heal entirely and then to learn to walk again, effortlessly.

Oh, there were days I longed to go back to my *normal* life, as I knew it. Yet, in the back of my mind, I also understood that my life would never be that same *normal* again. Somehow, I knew I had to find the joy, strength, and conviction of purpose to create a *new normal* for myself. I had to face this head-on and embrace it, or it was going to adversely affect the Remlee that I knew and the person my family loved. Given that, I came to the conclusion that I wasn't going to wait until my life wasn't hard anymore before I decided to be happy. My time to act was NOW!

Growing up, my parents taught me that you can consciously change the way you think about something before it becomes your reality, *if* you make up your mind to do so. Perception is everything, and how you think and feel is ultimately your choice. So, I chose to regard the entire *experience* as an *opportunity* in my life, rather than an obstacle that got in the way of my life. I recognized that I was so much more than the *bad* thing that happened to me, and I began to turn what could have been a negative situation into a positive solution.

I took a hard look at what was happening in my life since my injury was keeping me homebound 24/7. One of the first things I discovered was that I was comfortable being by myself. This was such an eye-opening revelation for me. I never enjoyed being alone or doing anything by myself before. My dad would always tell me, “If you really want to go somewhere or do something and you can’t find a friend to go with, then be your own best friend and go with *you!*” Dad would be so proud if he could see me now—home alone and enjoying my own company!

I was a captive audience with plenty of time on my hands. I stopped trying to figure things out and *finally* just let go and let God. I acquired a new love for singing and enjoyed doing crafts. It wasn't long before I found joy in most everything I did. Ultimately, I desired to be the best I could be in my situation. I would remind myself that it’s the process and not the event that I needed to focus on. This wasn’t a race, but a rite of passage I needed to go through to walk tall and proud (once again) before the end of summer.

Physical therapy had become a bi-weekly excursion as those weeks slipped into months. When the time drew near for me to start putting weight on my leg once again, I was having mixed feelings. *No! I’m NOT ready. What if my knee doesn’t support me? What if I fall again? What if I have to start this all over? What if, what if, what if ...* then, I found my strength from within these mighty statements of truth:

- Be strong and carry on, no matter what you face.
- Trust that things will always work out.

- Keep showing up.
- Strive for excellence, not perfection.
- Choose JOY!
- Don't let anyone take your joy.
- Stay the course. You got this!

And, I did it! It took me two weeks to graduate from my *chariot* to using a cane, which I lovingly nicknamed "Michael." I felt such excitement when I *walked* into my orthopedic doctor's office on my own *before* the end of August. It was pure joy!

Blessings can be found in life experiences. Today, I have a beautiful deck where my ramp once stood, and I seamlessly breezed through the solitude of COVID-19. I realize that the greatest teacher in life is life itself, and there is nothing constant but change. Life will continue to throw challenges our way, and it's up to us to use the knowledge and lessons gained from the past. I am definitely better equipped, now that joy has become the *motor* of my existence and *I am* in the driver's seat.

About Remlee

Remlee Peck, MEd, has been an inspiration to people of all ages for more than 35 years. She is a strong supporter and advocate for children and their families, and she assists individuals and small groups with their personal growth and well-being. Remlee's experience as a psychiatric social worker, lifelong educator, school counselor, and author has led the way for the creation and success of her business, Coaching You For Change.

As a life coach, Remlee provides support to many who experience personal, emotional, or behavioral concerns. She incorporates various mind-body wellness techniques and strives to offer unique alternatives to transform customary ways of thinking.

Remlee is a motivational speaker who offers participants their own *Keys for Success*. She leads numerous seminars and workshops, both locally and internationally, on a wide variety of topics.

Being a master gardener, Remlee loves sharing her talents with others. She organizes interactive group activities on gardening and coordinates kid-friendly class events.

Connect with Remlee

Website: www.coachingyouforchange.com

Email: coachingyouforchange@gmail.com

Facebook: https://facebook.com/coachingyouforchange

Instagram: https://instagram.com/coachingkids4change

Fulfilling the Dream

Huong Phung

"Live for the moment; love every minute."

~ Remlee Peck

I was born in the small city of Nam Dinh of Vietnam. When I was four years old, my family decided to flee the country on a boat, along with hundreds of other families. We were on the sea for close to a month.

My parents told us that, at one point, they ran out of food and supplies, and they had to go along the border of China to beg the locals for food. Somehow, we ended up in a Hong Kong refugee camp along with thousands of other Vietnamese families.

Even though I was little, I still remember my childhood in the camp quite clearly. I remember that this was our home, surrounded by barbed wire. I also remember our playground where we played hide and seek and did jumping jacks with our friends, our familiar alleys where we cooked our food on a hot charcoal fire (this is where my love for cooking comes from), our public bathroom where we cleaned dishes and took showers, and our hard bunk beds where we slept, ate, and shared with hundreds of other families.

So many lives ended right in front of me as people refused to be imprisoned and tried to escape. Food was limited. I remember seeing people fight over a piece of pork fat, but I also have fond memories of my favorite meal on Sundays, when we had Spam. After seven years of living in the camp, we were forced to go back home to Vietnam. A lot of people refused to go back, and I remember the police throwing tear grenades at us.

My parents volunteered to go back since my brother was only three years old. It seems like we were out of hope for the life that we dreamed of, but somehow, we kept that hope going, I thank God for my mom, as on the last day before we went back, she signed up for a program that gave us a chance to get to America one day. Even though we had nothing but struggles and hardships, we were so happy that we had each other, our family. The words we lived for were "hope" and "freedom," and we were willing to sacrifice for it.

This year marks 27 years since we left the Hong Kong refugee camp and returned to Vietnam. It also marks 25 years of living in America. Looking back, I am so thankful to this day that we are alive and we are here in America, the land of freedom and the land of opportunity. This is the reason why I am so passionate about the Nourish the Children Program and feel blessed to have an opportunity to give back and be a voice for less fortunate children!

Even with the struggles of my childhood, one of the hardest moments in my life was going through my divorce. No one ever gets married believing that it is going to end. I always thought of one day writing a book about my interracial love story. My husband and I had to overcome the challenges of being together: me being raised in a traditional Vietnamese family and him being outside of my race. Our relationship taught me to fight for what I truly believed in, what you could call *true love,* the love that was going to last forever. But it didn't work that way. I always wanted a family where my daughter would grow up in a loving home. Then there I was, with my 18-month-old daughter, and my marriage was falling apart.

Anything and everything you experience in life has purpose; it has brought you to where you are now. Part of me felt ashamed, guilty, embarrassed, alone, wanting to make it work, while part of me wanted to stand up for what I believe in, to have the freedom to be who I am, and to not lose myself in the marriage. I truly believe God can turn the broken pieces into something beautiful, those special defining moments that turn your life around.

I still remember that night, holding my daughter as she slept. I was at my lowest, and I started praying and reaching out to God for help, to show me the way. At that moment, I surrendered to him and asked him for guidance. I felt so connected to the divine and had faith that I was being protected. I felt safe sharing my pain with him, knowing that he will take care of me no matter what. From that day forward, my faith grew stronger.

I moved out of the house and rented my first apartment. I barely knew anyone in town and was on my own journey of healing. I became a single mom, living far away from my family. Not seeing my daughter every day was so difficult, and still is. Most of the time, I feel so lonely. It's so hard to sleep at night without her. I refuse to allow myself to be a victim, though. I know God has a bigger purpose for me, and I deserve better. It was the best decision ever to not focus on my sorrow but to focus on sharing and healing others. I have experienced that nothing lasts forever; time heals the wounds in my heart. Only I can overcome it and step forward!

Women and sisters, love yourself. Don't sacrifice for someone and lose yourself. Every day, love yourself more, do what you like, and dedicate yourself to something that allows you to have peace in life. Let go and forgive. It is very difficult, but send good thoughts to those who have hurt you, those who have come and gone. I gathered my courage the other day to apologize to those who have played that role in my life for the things I may have done to hurt them. After that, I felt relieved. I thank them for their lessons, thank them for helping me grow and become stronger.

God has taught me to find simple joy in each day. I am very grateful for my daughter Sydney, who is my greatest joy, inspiration, and biggest blessing. We enjoy each moment we have together, whether simply having a picnic at the park after school, laying under the trees, looking up at beautiful blue sky, singing and learning Vietnamese songs together, watching Disney movies, singing her lullaby as she falls asleep, or going downtown for free concerts. Whenever I get to be with her, I make sure I give her extra hugs and kisses and tell her how much I love her. Her smile and laugh always brighten my day!

Five years ago, I started my cooking class in the tiny kitchen of my first apartment in Erie, Pa. This place has given me shelter and a chance to start living my life all over again. I picked this place because God spoke to me in the kitchen, "Give thanks to the Lord for he is good, and his love endures forever." I believe there will always be a second chance to recreate your life, even though sometimes things get tough, but I always look up, smile, and give thanks.

I am grateful, as I count great memories with friends who have come to visit, who have gathered here for cooking classes, spontaneous soup pop-ups, ladies' spa nights, vision board nights, etc. I've made so many wonderful divine connections. Without these, I would never have gotten the chance to travel to so many places (earned through my online business), visiting my team in Europe, going on my first missionary trip to the Dominican Republic, starting my Vietnamese cooking classes, building a community to help feed more malnourished children, or sharing my passion for empowering more women to go after their dreams.

I have created a big family of beautiful brothers and sisters. I never feel alone. I was so fortunate to meet the most amazing, genuine, supportive groups of friends from the Single Mom's Empowerment Group and the Coffee Club Divas. I say thank you to all my ladies, my friends who were there for me through thick and thin throughout my journey. You all truly made an impact on my life. You are queens, warriors, fighters, winners, and role models in my eyes; these women are living proof that anything is possible if you have a big dream and a big *why!* I am so blessed to learn from each and every one of you. Thank you for sharing your story, knowledge, and wisdom with me and for being part of my life. You were there for me during my worst time. I truly believe there are reasons for the people you've met in your life. Whether good or bad, I am thankful for them!

When they eat my soup, my friends often call it, "healing soup." They say, "Your soup can create world peace." I am actually most at peace with myself when I savor the soup, so I agree! Worries go away, and nothing else matters. This is where Huong's Healing Kitchen comes from. I heal others through my food and my story. I feel so blessed and joyful during those times. It feels liberating! Preparing food and feeding people brings nourishment, not only to our bodies, but to our spirits. Feeding people is a way of loving them, in the same way that feeding ourselves is a way of honoring our own creativity and genuineness. Food is symbolic of love and sharing love with others! I breathe faith and hope into women, inspiring them to follow their dreams of becoming independent women entrepreneurs through health, beauty, cooking, and transformation. GOD FIRST!

Family is important to me, especially my daughter Sydney. Every day is a new chance to make a difference and brighten someone's day! Be the force for good, a voice for children and women, and living a driven, purposeful life!

My dream one day is to have a space, a kitchen where everyone is welcome. It's a place of love, acceptance, empowerment, and inspiration called Huong's Healing Kitchen. You will leave happier than when you came in, and you will feel inspired to do something for others.

Women and children have always been my passion for what I'm doing. I am a proud ambassador for the Nourish the Children Program, feeding malnourished children monthly. I love to bring people together who have each other's back, and I love good healthy food, good vibes, and good company! It brings me so much joy, happiness, and fulfillment. Today, I offer private one-on-one or group cooking classes, private Asian hot pot/BBQ dinners, small pop-up impromptu dinners, and community outreach.

I hope some part of my story has inspired you to never give up on your hopes and dreams and to continue searching for your true happiness. I also hope that after reading my story and pondering these questions, you are ready to make that change and fulfill the passion and joy in your life.

About Huong

Huong Phung operates a global business in beauty and nutrition, partnering with Nu Skin Enterprises for the last 12 years. She also offers Vietnamese cooking classes and created Cooking with purpose-Nourish the Children, a group that helps drive nutritious Vitameal Rice donations to malnourished children in third world countries. Huong's passion is helping to feed malnourished children locally and globally. She is building a community and a family of like-minded, kind-hearted, and compassionate individuals to be a force for good in the world. Helping women and children has always been her passion, and she is a proud ambassador for Nourish the Children. She also created Huong's Healing Kitchen to help heal others through food and her story.

Connect with Huong

Facebook: https://www.facebook.com/Huonghealingkitchen

Email: huonghealingkitchen@gmail.com

Sustaining Contentment: Keeping What Really Matters

Cynthia Primm

Let the light illuminate your path
And each step that you take,
On the road crowded or less traveled
Never a mistake.
Your journey is your journey
A judge no man can be,
Just keep moving forward
And build from your history
Of lessons learned and tears you've shed
And dreams you've held inside
Let the light illuminate your path
And it will be your guide.
For you are worthy, you are all
That made you who you are today
This is your time, your best life yet
For joy will meet you on your way.

~ From *I found My Joy* (Cynthia Primm)[11]

What a story to tell ... of those clinking tin cans of fear, despair, tears, and pain, tied to me like the back of a wedding car. Outrunning your beginnings, cutting the cord to them, or releasing hold of the rudder that spins you in circles can be daunting, I know. Each of us has our own journey, bringing us to a place of knowing: knowing everything will be OK, knowing we

---

[11] Cynthia Primm – Women Beyond Breaking, https://womenbeyondbreaking.com/gurus/cynthia-primm/

have the strength not only to survive, but to thrive. I've often said that I feel like a vessel of lessons. They seem to come continuously, and with each one, I hope to finally be so full of them there isn't room for any more. But I can see in every ounce of my being that each lesson has helped me grow. I have learned so much about my resilience, my persistence, and my determination. I am grateful for this journey, and even more grateful to have strong mentors, women friends, and counselors to guide me along the way. They have helped me to have a better life, day by day.

My journey began in a very broken, dysfunctional home where abuse, chaos, and chemical dependency abounded. I began writing at the age of ten to get the pain I was feeling out of me. I cycled from despair to denial, endlessly, and wanted only to feel loved. By the age of 16, I was a legally emancipated minor living with my aunt. At 18, I followed the map programmed inside of me and went to college, funding my education and my own life.

A year after graduation, I married, had three children, and built a life and a successful career—all while silently struggling with never feeling like I was enough. Those closest to me knew of my struggles with self-esteem, but to the outside world, I looked like I checked all the boxes of a successful woman. Being a mom to my three children, and being able to raise them differently than I was, is a blessing I am still very thankful for today. Now grown, they are living their own lives, following their own paths, and on journeys that I celebrate ... and occasionally join.

And then, as an empty nester, wisdom finally found me. After years of being *all* things to *all* people, I now considered being *all* things to me! I created the following construct to help me focus on four things that I can control, and once I learned to release everything else, I found sustainable contentment. As I've explored each element below, I've analyzed my discontent and what is happening to cause it, and then, I step back to consider the information. Once I do, I shift to realign, again and again. This is my new pattern—my new cycle—one that is fulfilling beyond measure.

The Construct Questions:

Do I love where I live?

Do I love what I do?

Do I love who I love?

Do I love myself?

Loving Where You Live

I am a Pisces—a water baby. I have always found myself at complete peace by any body of water. And while I've known this, and traveled many times to be by the water, I had never lived on the water or anywhere with a view of a large body of water. It was only in my 50s that I resolved to always live on or near the water because now I know ... I can make that choice.

If you want to love where you live, ask yourself, where do you feel most at peace? Where do you feel the most nourished in your soul? Make a plan for living there. You may not be able to move right away, but if you commit to filling your soul in this way, and take steps toward that goal, you will find opportunities to take you there. I have lived by the water for the past five years now, and realizing how deeply I connect to who I am when I replenish my soul by the water, I can tell you personally, *loving where you live* matters!

Loving What You Do

This one is tricky for most of us. What we do—our careers, our source of income—does not always equate to our calling. I've been a successful human resources leader for over three decades. The deeply ingrained career map has now turned into a constantly recalculating GPS. As an empty-nester, I can release the heavy bonds of responsibility for others, and with reduced expenses—by attrition or on purpose—I find my choices for work expand. The COVID-19 pandemic accelerated the importance of loving what I do. Because work takes up so many waking hours, I found myself wanting every minute to count ... more than ever before. I began to understand the value that joyful work can have in my life. So now, I teeter between two worlds: the one that I am known for and have built my career around in human resources, and the other vocation that involves curating an online community for women where I write inspirational blogs and books and coach and mentor women. One day, when I am finally ready to give up the tether to human resources (where I do, by the way, get to at least mentor and coach women) and jump with both feet into my calling, then I will have truly mastered this category. For now, I do whatever I can to fill my time (outside of traditional HR leadership) with efforts that fuel my calling.

Loving Who You Love

Being raised by a narcissistic abusive father and an alcoholic mother appears to have predispositioned me to fight for love and attention and not readily recognize red flags in my personal relationships. While these love lessons have been the toughest so far, they are also the lessons that allowed me to let go of old patterns when I was willing to learn from them. In my adult years, I spent six years in an emotionally abusive and controlling relationship, after being married for 24 years to someone who was, thankfully, the exact opposite. Imagine me, after decades away from the abusive house I grew up in, finding myself engulfed in old patterns and old feelings, with an untenable desire to keep it a secret! As I processed all my feelings when this six-year relationship ended, I first asked myself the question, *Why did I stay so long?* As I considered this, so many answers came to me: I didn't want to face being wrong about my choice to enter the relationship; I wanted to *be enough* to change the abuser; and I didn't want to be alone. Those answers led me to a better question, *Why did I stay after the first incident of abuse?*

And then, it came to me ... with great clarity! The first time the abuse happened in this relationship, it took me by surprise and at such a deep level that it jarred my *emotional muscle memory*. I didn't even realize that it was still living inside me. At that moment, I became a young girl again and all the protective measures I used as a young child came back to me, like people pleasing, putting myself aside, becoming numb, living in denial, and trying to manage the perception others had of me. All these responses kept me stuck. The beautiful lesson in this is realizing I am not a young girl anymore, but a woman full of wisdom, resources, and love. And if any other triggers occur in my life, I'll be ready to take my stand.

Patterns appear in relationships to point you to areas where you need more work. When you recognize what you are feeling is not new, pay attention because the pattern shows you that you need to keep growing in that area. If a pattern keeps resurfacing, take time to step back, journal what feels like it's on repeat in your relationships, and ask yourself *when* and *where* the pattern first began. Most likely, with an honest and fearless deep dive, you will be able to see that you are a different person than you were, you have more clarity about what you want in your life, and you know better what you deserve. You deserve (at minimum) to be loved how you love others, not necessarily how you learned in your early years, especially if it was dysfunctional. While this has been the area I have struggled with the most, it is also the area I am most committed to ensuring is a safe, nurturing, passionate, and invigorating place for me now. I accept no excuses—nothing less—because learning how to love myself first, as the adult woman I am today, is critically important to loving who I love well.

Loving Yourself

I am, and you are, fully in control of how much we love ourselves. Let that sink in. Find a quiet place to sit and take an inventory of how you are loving yourself in that moment. A long time ago, I realized I had automatic negative thoughts that would appear, like a tape playing in the back of my subconscious. I taught myself to identify those negative messages, turn a mirror back on them, and challenge myself to see if they were really true. Were they outdated? Did they come from a place in my childhood where the adults wallowed in hurt? Keeping yourself in the present while looking forward, taking the time for self-care, and throwing that recorded tape into the wind all put you on the path to loving yourself. I find vision boarding, repeating personalized daily affirmations, and being thankful in advance for what positive things I know are coming really settles and balances me.

We are a vessel of lessons made of clay that will break to make room for our growth. We are constantly putting the pieces back together, creating an even more beautiful vessel that will shatter with our next period of growth. We expand and grow throughout our lives, and we are walking, talking vessels of wisdom. Life is a continuous process of growth that encompasses doing the work needed in any one of the four areas I've described to maintain a healthy balance for our spirits to thrive. The world can be tough on us. We can be—and are—tougher!

I curate a website called Women Beyond Breaking. The title came out of decades of conversations with women who identify with *breaking*. For example, we deeply feel *break*-ups, and we *break* when we give birth. What if in this breaking, we were really like clay pots—vessels for lessons—where in breaking, we grow? The biblical meaning of "vessel" denotes a person God calls and uses who is receptive. Moving the focus from beyond breaking to growing and focusing on loving yourself, loving others, loving what you do, and where you live, creates the space for you to build sustainable contentment in your life.

Remember: it takes a village. Surround yourself with strong mentors, women friends, and counselors. You are in control of giving yourself what you need. You got this!

About Cynthia

Cynthia Primm resides in Pennsylvania. She holds a bachelor of science degree in business administration from Bryant College in Smithfield, R.I., and is a Wainwright Global certified life coach. Cynthia has spent most of her years as an empowering and impactful human resources leader and still works in that career today.

Continuing to be purpose-driven, Cynthia is also the founder of Women Beyond Breaking, an online community of women committed to empowering, encouraging, and equipping each other on the journey to live beyond brokenness. Cynthia is passionate about mentoring and coaching people—especially women—to continue to grow, learn, and live out the calling on their lives. She is the author of two books, *I'll Trade My Sorrow* and *I Found My Joy,* both available at www.womenbeyondbreaking.com.

Connect with Cynthia

Email: cynthiaprimm@womenbeyondbreaking.com

Facebook: https://www.facebook.com/womenbeyondbreaking/

Website: https://womenbeyondbreaking.com/

Nightmare to Daydream

Stephanie Reagle

"I am not what happened to me; I am what I choose to become."[12]

~ Carl Jung

There I was, sitting in the car with my mom at the CVS Pharmacy parking lot in my hometown. We both had a traumatizing night watching my stepdad grab my brother by the throat and slam him against the wall. My mom was in shock and exhausted, but there she was, taking me to pick out a gift for my friend's birthday party. "I can't take it anymore," I kept saying over and over again. Eventually, I built up the courage to tell my mom that my stepdad had been sexually abusing me for the last three years.

My mom did the best thing a mom could ever do in a situation like that, she believed me, and she fought for me. We went into the store to grab a gift and then headed home, pretending like nothing had happened. The tricky thing about these traumatizing, core memories is that life doesn't stop for us to process them. I had my friend's sleepover that Friday night, and Saturday morning, before the pancakes, my mom picked me up to talk to a caseworker and start the process of sending my stepdad away. I believe I was either 11 or 12. Later that day, the case worker and my mom confronted my stepdad, and he left to stay with his parents. It was the first night I slept in a long while.

---

[12] Carl Gustav Jung, Quote by Carl Gustav Jung: "I am not what happened to me, I am what I choos..." | Goodreads

After the examinations, the preliminary hearing, and the trial, I thought I could move on and pretend like nothing had happened. The thing about avoidance is that all you're doing is suppressing your emotions and feelings; you're not dealing with reality. I felt like I would be happy if I could pretend to be someone this didn't happen to, but I ended up causing myself more harm than good. I developed a habit that if I didn't agree with something, I played along to avoid an argument or avoid making the other person uncomfortable.

My mom let me take dance and speech forensics, try out for basketball, and be on the volleyball team, and I had a part-time job at 16. I hung out with friends on the weekends as I got older. I seemed like an average kid. If you didn't know what was going on behind closed doors. Somewhere in the timeline, I stopped processing what was happening, and survival mode was ignited.

I would try to find something to fill the void from feeling unworthy. I was entering my adolescent years, and I was always concerned about how I looked. I found myself making strict rules and punishments around what I ate. Underage drinking was common for high schoolers, and it was common to party and try drugs in college, so, I didn't think anything of it! Little did I know, things were bubbling up to the surface, making me want to escape my body and thoughts.

How did I overcome this huge life event that could have destroyed me? I stopped avoiding my insecurities and faults and started to embrace them. I strengthened my mind and stopped trying to be someone I wasn't. I decided that I was going to own this tragedy and give it a purpose! I started to chisel at the wall I had built around myself for the last ten years. The first moment I realized I needed to put this shame to rest was when I found out I was pregnant with my daughter.

I was only 19 years old and back home after my first year of college. I spent my summer working full-time as a teller at National Fuel and working weekends at Sparkling Ponds Winery.

My plan was to attend Indiana University of Pennsylvania's (IUP) nutrition program in the fall of 2013, but I needed to rehab my GPA first, meaning I would start at IUP in the spring of 2014. My plans shifted a bit when I found myself with sore boobs and a positive pregnancy test. For some reason, maybe the power of manifestation or the curse of having a daughter like me, I knew I was carrying a girl. Something about that connection made me feel hope, and, more importantly, *love*!

I never had plans to be a mom, and I was always scared of attachment after being hurt by the people I was supposed to trust. It was an emotional time, and the fluctuating hormones didn't help, but the connection I felt from her growing inside me revealed a part of myself I needed to nurture. From there, I decided to pursue an accounting and finance degree. It was a safe and secure career, and I could support my daughter and myself. I thought I was doing the right thing for my daughter, but I found myself stressed and depressed. I wasn't passionate about accounting, and that was teaching my daughter that passion didn't matter! My daughter was somewhere between one to two years old when I decided to quit school and take the management position at the winery I was working at until I knew what I wanted to do.

I wanted to teach my daughter that she could do anything she put her mind to, even if it was against the norm. I wanted her to follow her dreams! I was able to support us with my new position, but the stress was a lot to handle. Eventually, I yearned for a holistic lifestyle for myself and my daughter. After a month, I enrolled at Great Lakes Institute of Technology in their massage therapy program. I had never had a massage before. I was infatuated with how the profession helped people heal naturally.

We are constantly evolving into the person we are meant to be. Some things in life are out of our control, but what we do with those things determines our path. God, the Universe, a higher power, whatever you want to call it, has a plan for everyone. It's essential to allow yourself to be open and receptive to it.

Everything truly happens for a reason. Lorelai's biological dad was good friends with my abuser's son. I was 16 when I met him, and he knew what had happened to me. I felt accepted for what I had gone through. If it weren't for that connection, I wouldn't have Lorelai.

My daughter has taught me to lead by example. If I want my daughter to love herself unconditionally, I had to start loving myself. This little girl has brought so much adventure to my life! If I weren't a single mom, I wouldn't have had the opportunity to rekindle my relationship with my partner, Joseph. We first met when he was 21, and I was 17, but eventually went our separate ways. After six years, we went on our first date! If I didn't have Joseph, I wouldn't have my son, Baker. If I didn't have the three most valuable people in my life, I wouldn't have this family who has taught me to love and be loved in return. Do you see? Everything truly happens for a reason. It has not been a solely beautiful, straightforward journey to get to this point. I spent many years being angry, trying to process my trauma, but I know I wouldn't have had that pull to learn massage without this abuse. I regained my power by learning the art of intentional, healing touch.

You have to seek out and choose joy actively. The more you work for it, the easier it will become to find and experience joy. My mindset is what keeps me on track. Instead of asking myself *why* this was happening to me, I started figuring out *how* it could work *for* me. I consider myself to have a unique perspective. I am sensitive to particular situations related to my rough upbringing and the abuse I experienced. But, if I spend the rest of my life feeling sorry for myself, I will die a bitter, resentful person; that is not why we are here on this Earth.

I thought I would be taking this chapter to the grave with me. I didn't want to be seen as a victim. The truth is, I *was* a victim, but that doesn't mean I have to wear that title the rest of my life! Sometimes you need to call it out to finally end the thought-cycle. You choose who you become. I decided to be a mom (they chose me). I chose to open myself to love. I decided to use my gift of healing touch and knowledge to help other women find pain and stress relief. *I chose to be a survivor*! What will you choose?

I bet you're all wondering what happened to my abuser. He was sentenced to three to ten years (we were reassured he would be getting eight); however, he received an early dismissal due to good behavior. What's even crazier? Despite the letters we sent in, he was allowed to live in the same town I did, but I wasn't allowed to know his address ... for *his* safety. He was allowed at the school, would walk by our house, and show up at my brother's work. Well, years later, he was murdered. Rumor has it he was fooling around with the neighbor's girlfriend, and the guy found out. Next thing you know, double murder-suicide.

Two life-changing attitudes to remember:

1. Karma is real. If you put good out there, it will come back. You have to trust.
2. Actively choose joy. The more you look for joy, the more it will appear.

About Stephanie

Stephanie Reagle is a mother, partner, licensed massage therapist, and Lake Erie Massage Therapy owner. She grew up with a love of dance and volleyball. She has a family that will bust a move to keep the good energy flowing! Joseph, her partner, keeps her grounded, safe, and laughing. They enjoy building a life together, nurturing each other— especially in hardships—and navigating parenthood.

As Stephanie grows, she gets more assertive in her health and self-awareness. She uses her gift and knowledge of massage therapy to help women suffering from chronic pain and stress and works with some of the area's best yoga and meditation practitioners. Her mission is to help other women along their wellness journey and to bring to light that food, movement, emotional health, and spirituality all work together to provide a vibrant life!

Stephanie believes in dedication, hard work, and happiness. She is learning grace and patience. Her goal is to raise her children, alongside her partner, with the belief that they can do anything they set their minds to, to be kind to themselves and others, and to have a good sense of humor!

Connect with Steph

Email: stephreagle.lmt@gmail.com

Website: www.lakeeriemassagetherapy.com

Facebook: www.facebook.com/lakeeriemassagetherapy

Instagram: www.instagram.com/lakeeriemassagetherapy

The Whisper

Theresa Ream

"When someone walks into our lives and opens a door of opportunity, it is our duty to walk through it."

~ Theresa Ream

Soul's Purpose

I truly believe that most people go to their graves never knowing their soul's purpose.

How many times have you heard women say, "I wish I knew my life's purpose?" They may even say things like, "I wish I could find my calling; this job is not me; I always thought I would be, well, you name it: a nurse, a coach, a world traveler, or an entrepreneur living their dream!" I can tell you from experience that they fell into the trap of living someone else's version of their lives.

What does it feel like to neglect your soul? Life can feel uneventful, unsatisfying, and like something is missing. You may even experience imposter syndrome, feel like you're not good enough, or you miss the rush that comes from doing what you love. The list can be long. Isn't it time to find your soul's purpose? You've been putting it off way too long. My chapter is about a warrior's call to action. It's time to fight the fear of the unknown, the opinions of others, and most dangerously, your own negative opinions of yourself. It's time to take care of yourself. It's time to find real joy!

The Small Whisper

Maybe the whisper started when you were very little and unconditioned by the judgements of others. You knew what you wanted. You knew who you were in your bones. You were sure-footed and unencumbered, a force of lightness with an internal fortitude. The whisper was always close by, nudging you forward in your life with good feelings about how you show up. For me, I love knowing, connecting, and envisioning better lives for others. I innately notice things about people and intuitively see directions they should take. I knew I could help and guide people when I grew up, and one day, I told my mom, "I'm going to be a psychiatrist or a therapist." My mom wasn't mean, in fact she was one of the most loving moms I have ever known, but her casual response killed my dream. She said, "If you do, you will find out I'm crazy." *Crazy? My Mom?* The thought burned in me and sent a chill through me at the same time. She might have been joking, but my little girl's heart tucked that calling away in a box that I kept hidden for a long time. Even so, I would occasionally peek in at it, keeping my dream alive. I wanted to help others live their best lives. That one statement changed the way I felt about myself. I suddenly didn't trust my judgment of who I really was anymore.

I always wondered about whispers ... shouldn't something so important for us to know at least be a shout?

But, no, we all must work to get past the loud chatter of the world and be alert to the messages we send ourselves. I believe the whisper becomes more prevalent as we get older and have not yet tapped into our soul's purpose. The lack of movement toward our destiny finds us lacking in other areas too and can manifest in eating disorders, poor communication, failed or bad relationships, an unwillingness to try new things, unreasonable fears, and/or not following our instincts.

So, what can we do to put ourselves on the path to our souls' purpose? Life wants to be expressed through us, and energy flows out of us to others when we are in alignment with our gifts and purpose. If that energy from Divine isn't flowing outward, it gets stuck in us and causes blocks, exhausts us, or worse, makes us ill.

Navigating Life

You must become proficient in navigating your life. Navigation is following your internal compass, getting in touch with your deepest held values, and continuing to course correct to align with your true self (not someone else's rendition of who you are). Your inner navigation isn't set up to see from start to finish; it's like driving in the dark with the headlights allowing you to see only a short distance at a time. Eventually, you will get there. Life is like a thick forest with dense trees and many paths: some cold and dark, others sunny and warm. Your soul's purpose will feel expansive with possibilities, but the wrong path will feel restrictive, generating more questions than answers in your gut. Your inner navigation is steered by self-trust and sometimes coaxed by a good and trusted coach. Look for clues to find your purpose: what excites you, what gives you energy, and what do you love? What do people notice you are good at?

When I was a sophomore in high school, I got the chance to take some college courses in the summer. I took creative writing and music. I loved writing; it felt great. I often felt like I was in some type of life-force flow when writing, even sage-like. The professor said, "Theresa, you are a good writer. I want you to pursue writing more." My writing was over by the end of that summer. Why? Because I thought I wasn't smart enough. After all, my much older brother was literally a rocket scientist, and I never felt smart enough next to him. How could I be a writer?

Comparison thwarts our navigation and keeps us from finding our soul's purpose. Most of us have, or have had, a never-ending good-girl checklist. As we check items off the list, we think, *Now I will be valued.* But it's no one else's job to value us; this job belongs to us alone. Only when we learn how to do this for ourselves will the value from others flow freely, allowing us to navigate our lives toward our purpose.

The Work Ahead

After the whisper is identified as a calling, and you learn to trust yourself, then what? Well, to change one thing is to change many. There is a reaction to every action, known as cause and effect, and you want to be on the cause side of the equation. That means taking responsibility for everything. If someone mistreats you, look at the cause and how you could have mitigated it in some way. It means never being the victim; instead, striving for change, learning, and growing from your circumstances. I know it's easier said than done. I think that's what Viktor Frankl, the well-known holocaust survivor and psychologist, must have done as a prisoner of war amid torchers. He was known for his survival mindset as shared in one of his most well-known works, *Man's Search for Meaning.*[13] You will need to challenge how you think and beef up your mental fortitude to attune to and follow your soul's purpose. My experience is that you will also need a great coach mentor.

Self-Growth Leads to Self-Discovery

Personal growth isn't about taking information, learning from it, and then playing someone else's game; it's about giving to others because you know you have something to offer to every single person you meet. Personal growth is an outward expression of the wisdom you learned and earned. I love personal growth; I always have. The thrill of becoming better each day excites me, and, in this quest, I was able to recognize that the childhood whisper was in fact a calling I began to perfect.

My husband and I are the founders of several successful multimillion-dollar businesses. We started our first one 42 years

---

[13]Viktor Frankl, https://psycnet.apa.org/record/1992-98457-000

ago. At 16, I wrote out a complete description of my dream husband. Six months later, Terry, the flesh and blood man I described, walked out a door that I was entering. I knew he was my man. I still hold the vision of him walking through that door in my mind so clearly.

We are both cut from the same cloth: we are action oriented, people loving, and thrill seeking. We love too much and forgive too quickly. Life wasn't always easy for us. We fought hard to stay together through addiction, clung close to each other during a cancer battle (with a 3% survival rate), and suffered through addiction with our children, but I wouldn't change a thing about our relationship. The battles we fought together made us who we are today, and joy fills our lives, our homes, and our businesses. I love our roles as entrepreneurs and employers in our community. I love the excitement of being an entrepreneur, but there was always something missing, something to call my very own. I wanted to personally help others live their best lives just like my childhood whisper. All these years, my personal growth journey has led me to this calling.

This year, I decided to take the leap into my calling. I have worked on certifications to facilitate my coaching journey and have named my business Feminine W.I.L.E.S (Women Inspired Leadership Empowering Service). I am excited to see what this new chapter in my life brings. I am even more excited about the women I will help in their journey to grow, blossom, and gain confidence and clarity around their souls' purpose, naturally improving themselves, their businesses, teams, and communication skills. In my gut, I know that in helping others, I will be the one who is finally made whole.

About Theresa

Theresa Ream is the founder of several multimillion-dollar businesses known as the Ream Companies and has over 42 years of business success. She is known for founding the largest minority woman-owned restoration company on the central coast and beyond. The Ream Companies include Disaster Kleenup Specialists, FRSTeam, Flooring America's Floor Store USA, and Cypress Design & Build.

Theresa is also the founder of Feminine W.I.L.E.S lifestyle business consultants, and her passion is helping established CEOs and entrepreneurs. She utilizes her strong organizational, financial, marketing, and nurturing skills to help women eliminate overwhelm and get clarity in their businesses by coaching them in systems, marketing, and building happy teams. Theresa believes you must build the woman to build the business.

Theresa is also skilled in running multigenerational family-owned businesses. She's been honored with the Best Woman

Owned Business on the Monterey Peninsula award and the Best Minority Owned Business of Monterey award, along with being named The Woman of the Year by The Professional Women's Network of Monterey.

Theresa is a community leader, speaker, bestselling author, blogger, writer (as a business expert) for *Marketing, Media & Money Magazine*, podcast guest, co-host of The Professional Women's Network Ask The Expert podcast, as well as the current President of the Professional Women's Network of the Monterey Peninsula.

When Theresa is not serving in her business and community, she is an avid reader and traveler, loves bootcamp-style workouts and riding her bike, and is happily raising her 12-year-old grandson, Cash, with her husband Terry.

Connect with Theresa

Facebook: https://www.facebook.com/theresa.ream.98

LinkedIn: https://www.linkedin.com/in/theresaream

Empower Your Mind, Transform Your Reality

Taira Ruzzi

"It is during our darkest moments that we must focus to see the light."[14]

– Aristotle Onassis

This quote has been a constant source of inspiration for me, helping me maintain a positive mindset throughout my life. I have faced numerous health issues and traumatic events, but I am grateful for my loving parents who have always gone above and beyond to address my health concerns. Many people have not been as fortunate in that regard. Due to my severe asthma and weak immune system since birth, I easily fall ill, and even a common cold can leave me bedridden for weeks. As a child, I was frequently sick and had to stay home often. When I couldn't accompany my parents to work, I would stay with my grandparents, and was occasionally watched by a teenager in our neighborhood. As I grew older, my family and I moved away from my hometown in Florida, settling in Pennsylvania, in my mom's hometown. Before I knew it, I was an adult embarking on my college journey.

Driven by my fascination with the subject, I decided to enroll in a psychology class during college. It proved to be an engaging topic for me, and during the course, we explored trauma and the

[14]Aristotle Onassis." *Good News Network*, 16 June 2023, www.goodnewsnetwork.org/aristotle-onassis-quote-about-focus/.

brain's ability to suppress memories that are too distressing. I listened to many gut-wrenching stories. Even though the stories were sad, the class perfectly aligned with my interests. I found great joy in learning about the incredible capabilities of the human mind. However, life took an unexpected turn.

Despite things seemingly going well, I experienced a complete physical and mental breakdown. It was during this time that a deeply traumatic and shameful memory resurfaced—a memory I had long suppressed and had no recollection of until that moment. Beginning around the age of seven, my male teenage neighbor had been sexually assaulting me, and I had no idea how long it went on. Racing thoughts and overwhelming self-doubt consumed me. I grappled with questions of blame, wondering if I was somehow responsible for what happened. It was an internal battle that seemed never-ending.

Finally, I made the decision to confide in my mother, even though it was difficult. In a state of hysteria, struggling to find my voice, I shared everything—the remorse, shame, guilt, and self-blame. My self-worth hit rock bottom, leaving me feeling incredibly vulnerable and confused as I sat on my parents' bed with my mom. She hugged me tightly, grasped my hand, and looked me in the eyes. She explained that I was far too young at the time to comprehend whether the situation was right or wrong. “It was the responsibility of the teenage boy to make the proper choices and know right from wrong. You are not a bad person because of what happened,” she explained to me. Her words brought reassurance and a new understanding of the situation.

I took time to reflect and untangle the complexities in my mind. I yearned to move forward, to live a life where this memory didn't define me. Gradually, I reached a better place mentally, where my mind found happiness once again. However, not long after, as I sat in my car after buying groceries, I decided to check my phone. Opening Facebook and scrolling through my feed, I was struck with disbelief—in my suggested friends' list was the person who sexually assaulted me. It felt like an inescapable reminder. Seeing his name and photo was the last thing I needed. Once again, I had to confront this ordeal in my mind, and the resurfacing trauma took a toll on me. I realized that some wounds can only heal with time and conscious effort.

Determined not to let this experience dictate my life, I delved into self-exploration, discovering what brought me joy and happiness. I made the decision not to let this experience continue affecting me as it had in the past. A quote from Dr. Levine resonated with me during my healing journey, "Trauma is a fact of life. It does not have to be a life sentence."[15]

Self-reflection helped me to find joy in life, myself, and others. I asked myself, *What truly makes me happy?* I started exploring my hobbies and interests. Additionally, I found solace in listening to inspirational podcasts and incorporating regular workouts into my routine. Being active helped me process my thoughts and emotions, and every time I left the gym, I felt an invincible sense of resilience.

Music has always been an outlet for me. Whether I blared it through my speakers or sang along to songs that resonated with my experiences, the beats and vibrations became a saving grace. Above all, I held onto faith in myself and never lost sight of my true identity. Trauma can be stealthy, surfacing unexpectedly later in life, which certainly surprised me. However, I realized that personal growth is an ongoing journey. By embracing continuous learning, growth, and keeping our hearts and minds open, we can transcend the trauma and pain we've endured.

Remember, this is your story, your legacy. You possess the power to achieve anything as long as you believe in yourself. Know that I am sending love to you and wholeheartedly believe in you.

---

[15] Dr. Peter Levine, "'trauma Is a Fact of Life. It Does Not Have to Be a Life Sentence.'" *Jennifer Nurick*, 20 Sept. 2021,www.jennynurick.com/trauma-is-a-fact-of-life-it-does-not-have-to-be-a-life-sentence/.

Thank you for reading my story. I hope sharing my experience can help you transform some area of your life.

About Taira

Taira Ruzzi, is an entrepreneur, who, at the young age of 27, owns her own spa aesthetics and semi-permanent makeup business. She helps people feel beautiful, confident in their own skin, and more youthful through a variety of services such as facials, full body waxing, lash extensions, microblading, brow tinting, brow lamination, lash lift and tints ... and hopefully more in the future! She has been a licensed cosmetologist since 2016 and dabbled in all areas of cosmetology to find her niche. Taira has worked for high-end spas, providing a full range of hair and nail services, men's services, and much more. She fell in love with the esthetics part of the business and met some inspiring women—that's when everything took off!

Originally born in Florida, Taira moved back and forth from Florida to Pennsylvania many times through her life. She considers herself a half-city, half-country girl. Growing up with a very open-minded family, Taira's seen a lot of different circumstances and is typically a sponge in the background soaking it all up. She considers herself an old soul. Despite being young and fighting the commonly held belief that you shouldn't leave a steady fulltime job for something risky, she chose to step into her spotlight and follow her dreams! She's always been told she can do whatever she sets her mind to ... and that stuck with her. Taira has always taken life by the horns and just goes for it! All she ever wants to do is spread love and positivity and help others. She hopes to inspire someone along the way!

Connect with Taira

Facebook: https://www.facebook.com/taira.ruzzi

Instagram: https://www.instagram.com/beautylabink/

Website: www.glowluxeerie.glossgenius.com

Email: tairaruzzi@gmail.com

The Gift

Ella Smith

"The Lord is close to the brokenhearted and saves those who are crushed in spirit."

Psalm 34:18 (NIV)

In February 2022, my husband, a city firefighter, came home from work after a 24-hour shift, complaining of an excruciating pain in his shoulder. A scan revealed a huge mass on his liver and other organs. After more tests, we were scheduled to see an oncologist. The day prior to our visit, we reviewed the MRI report at home. We prayed and went to bed.

The next morning, we faced reality—he was diagnosed with non-Hodgkin's lymphoma. My husband had quit smoking eight years prior to this diagnosis and lived a healthy lifestyle. We were shocked by the news. However, we were grateful for two things: Mikey didn't get a death sentence, *You have six months to live,* and it wasn't liver cancer. My husband, at age 46 took this news as God's call to have a grateful heart and the courage to fight.

Throughout the chemo treatments, Mikey continued to have a very positive attitude. He followed the doctor's orders, with healthy nutrition and daily exercise. We enjoyed spending time in nature and walking our dog, Finn. Most people didn't know he was sick, and we didn't advertise it. We continued our journey, uplifting each other, and praying for strength and courage.

Mikey completed his treatments at the end of June 2022. He was eager to get back to life and work. However, two weeks after his last chemo treatment, he started having some unexpected problems. On July 24, 2022, the true nightmare began. We were supposed to leave that day for an annual vacation. I will never forget the gut-wrenching feeling that something was terribly wrong. My husband wasn't acting like himself, and I thought he was having a stroke. I called 911, and the ambulance took him to the hospital. That's when I witnessed his first grand mal seizure. It was a terrifying experience. I felt so lost. I didn't understand what was happening and why.

A couple of weeks later, I noticed changes in my husband's memory. He got progressively worse, but the doctor said, "It is a normal side effect from the medication." But to me, it was not normal, nor was it just a side effect to be brushed off as nothing serious.

By God's grace, we attended my sister's wedding on August 13, 2022. The next day, Mikey ended up at the Cleveland Clinic, where we received a new diagnosis: CNS lymphoma, affecting the central nervous system. Mikey's cancer had spread to his brain. My mind was racing with terrifying thoughts. *Is this deadly? What's the treatment? Where do we go from here?*

The prognosis was very poor, but the doctors gave us hope. They stressed that he was a young and healthy firefighter with a strong will, and that he had a great chance of surviving. I hung onto the hope that my husband would survive. Hope in God was my strength.

Mikey required 24/7 care. Our lives were turned upside down, and a new hospital life began.

I was with him from morning to night. I spent some nights at the hospital and some at the hotel. Friends and family often encouraged me to take care of myself so I could care for Mikey. While in the hotel, I prayed and lamented to my Father in heaven. Each day, He provided me with enough strength to get me through our unimaginable circumstances.

Unfortunately, due to the cancer's location, my husband suffered from horrible insomnia and intense seizures, among other medical emergencies. He was like a toddler and a dementia patient combined. We didn't know what to do. So, we focused on one day at a time, trusting God's providence.

We continued to face many challenges. From August until November 2022, Mikey spent weeks at the Cleveland Clinic. It was during this time that I learned what it meant to be an advocate. I did a lot of research and prayed for God to help me ask the right questions.

At one point, I was asked to leave the ICU room by a nurse who didn't like my suggestion. I learned that day that I had a voice, and I had the courage to speak with the nursing supervisor. As someone who was hands-on with my husband's daily care, all I wanted to do was help him. So I spoke up.

Another time, my husband's condition worsened, and I continued to ask questions, challenging the doctors to stop medications that were not helpful nor needed. When they stopped the medications as I had requested, they discovered that Mikey was seizing, and the meds were masking what was really going on inside. I'm glad I listened to my gut feeling, and that I didn't give up.

As we spent weeks in the hospital, we often went outside or walked the halls. We were inseparable. We had such a strong, beautiful marriage and an unbreakable bond. I had married my soulmate.

I was glad that even though I was hurting tremendously, the peace God gave me was beyond understanding. He kept me going for Mikey. I felt discouraged at times, but God continued to provide me with the strength and faith each day to carry on.

We had many struggles, yet, we encountered many miracles. One day, I felt extremely overwhelmed as I was driving home for a hair appointment. I didn't feel right getting my hair done while my poor husband was in the hospital. Not only did the hairstylist do my hair for free, but I also received monetary gifts, retail discounts, and hugs from neighbors—all in the same day. I felt blessed. God extended his love and compassion toward me through others.

At the end of October 2022, we witnessed another miracle: my husband's condition improved, and we brought him home for his 47th birthday. We had a nice party outside, and the best gift of all was that it was 70° in Erie in October! What a blessing! Mikey loved the warm weather. He would often say, "I just wish for a nice, sunny day. It's not too much to ask for." That wish was granted to him that day.

In November 2022, we saw true glimpses of hope as he responded to treatments. After two months of insomnia, we had another miracle: Mikey started sleeping at night. God answered our prayers for sleep. Another blessing! We were the happiest when Mikey was home. The home environment did wonders for his mental and physical wellbeing.

Also, my desperate prayers to have quality time with my hubby were answered. We were able to go on a couple of dates, and we often walked the dog in our neighborhood and Presque Isle! I've asked God for these two simple things, and he granted them.

To our surprise, a month later, Mikey took another turn for the worse, and we were introduced to a clinical trial with the hope it could be a life-changing treatment. Although his health continued to be up and down, I felt he was mentally better. Mikey was a trooper and never complained. I believe God gave him an extraordinary inner strength.

The following months were a blessing because I got to see my husband returning to almost normal. His sense of humor and, in particular, his sarcastic comments, made me know Mikey was still himself. It was a blessing to be able to spend time with him, praying, talking about God, and watching our favorite shows. We had faith and prayed for a miracle, but God had a different plan, and Mikey's death came all too soon. The cancer that took his life was deemed occupational. It was hard to accept that the job he so loved was the reason for his premature death.

While in the hospital, during the last few hours of his life, Mikey was peaceful. He pointed to the sky as if to say, *It's my time.* I don't know what he saw, but he appeared at peace. It was such a sacred experience.

On the day he passed away, February 26, 2023, I only left the room for a moment. I was told Mikey opened his eyes, and as a tear fell down his face, he took his last breath. He didn't want me to see him go. I was crushed. My soulmate went to the Lord.

Through this experience, I no longer fear death. What I experienced during this horrific time was that as an end happens here, a glorious new life begins with God. Mikey is just in *another room,* close by and waiting for me. He is cancer free now and is truly joyful in God's arms. We were never promised a life without trouble, but we have God to help us through our darkest times.

After my husband passed, I received a grief box containing books and resources for widows. When I opened it, I saw the word "widow," and it terrified me. I was not ready to see that word. I wept for hours. My sorrow was deep and indescribable.

I can't explain the emptiness and the pain I felt. I relied on God's Word to encourage me daily. It's hard to find joy amid a heart full of enormous pain, so I choose to be thankful daily for the gift of our marriage and the memories we built.

This heart-wrenching experience has deepened my faith. I praise God for his amazing and abiding love as I heal through my grieving journey.

Life is a large puzzle. God sees the whole picture, but we only see a few pieces. It's hard to comprehend. Life may seem unfair, but God knows why and how the pieces unfold in our lives. In fact, God prepared me for Mikey's death without my knowing. In 2021, I signed up for online courses in Biblical counseling. These classes helped me tremendously and prepared me for the time of suffering and grief that was to follow.

As I grieve, it's very easy to get lost in negative thoughts, which can lead to despair and helplessness. For this reason, I joined a support group called GriefShare and was grateful for the opportunity to walk through this chapter of my life with others who understood my pain. Each day brings new challenges, but with intentionality, I choose to focus on joy and God's promises that he will be with me through this dark valley. In the last few months, the following Scripture passages have gotten me through the darkest of times, and they continue to uplift my spirit as I recite them often.

"... I will never leave you nor forsake you." (Joshua 1:5, NIV)

"The Lord is close to the brokenhearted and saves those who are crushed in spirit." (Psalm 34:18, NIV)

"But I trust in you, O Lord; I say, 'You are my God.' My times are in your hands; ..." (Psalm 31:14-15, NIV)

I start and end each day with God, and I am learning and accepting a new way of life without my soulmate, best friend, phenomenal husband, loving caretaker, handyman, and lover. God will see me through, though I'm still in shock and grieving as I write this story. It's only been a couple of months.

We had a wonderful 17 years together, 14 of them married. We were inseparable. We loved the beach, traveling, date nights, and our dog. We led a simple but happy life. I will forever be grateful for the gift of our strong and beautiful marriage: a rarity it seems, these days. I will always remember the good times. Our dream of retiring in the South was shattered, but cancer can't take my memories of the life we built. I know that with a strong community of friends, family, and my faith, I will be able to heal my broken heart.

I am forever grateful to my in-laws for their support and love throughout this journey. I couldn't have done it without their tremendous help. Mikey's fire station, Engine #11, (Erie, Pa.) and other stations provided so much support throughout his illness ... and they continue to do so. He was well loved by so many. I am humbled by the support and love I have received. It's such a strong brotherhood, and I am proud to be a part of this family. Mikey would have been proud, too. He absolutely loved his job and was humbled to serve our community.

I never realized, until now, how many lives he touched. He left a beautiful legacy. His genuine spirit, positive outlook on life, strong faith, and work ethic showed in his character and his love for life.

We continue to honor Mikey's life in many ways including placing a photo of him in a Pittsburgh restaurant, designing T-shirts in his honor, placing his helmet in his fire station, and more. Writing this story is another way I am honoring my husband.

You too can get through what seems impossible with faith, support, and deciding you will never give up, no matter the outcome. You are not alone. Grief, hardship, and life crises come in different ways. I'm working through my unbearable life-altering circumstance, and you can, too ... one day at a time.

Life is fragile. Don't wait to tell people you love them; do it now. Share your love and life with your family and friends. Love God and seek his help. It's available to all who ask.

That is one thing Mikey and I did all the time. We shared a life of love and God's grace, and we had the best adventure ever!

About Ella

Ella Smith emigrated from Poland at the age of 16. She was married for 14 years to firefighter Michael (Mikey) Smith, who died of occupational cancer in 2023. She lives in Erie, Pa., with her loving dog Finn. Ella is currently working on finishing a biblical counseling certification through the Institute of Nouthetic Studies. She has a marketing degree, with minors in psychology and management from Penn State, Behrend.

If you or someone you know is going through unbearable grief and loss, please use the following resources:

- Minister at your local church
- www.GriefShare.org

Connect with Ella

Email: elunia77@hotmail.com

Facebook: https://www.facebook.com/widowscorner7

Joy Restored

Linda Laird Staszewski

"Our best days are ahead of us, the gold, after being refined by fire looks pure and beautiful! Greater Glory is on the way!"[16]

~ Marcia Santos

Tom and I married in 1975 in Erie, Pa. We moved eight hours away for the first two years, and then moved closer to our families, just three hours away. We remained there for 25 years. We bought our first house, and got our beautiful dog, Ausia the Airedale. We were both working, and life was good!

We enjoyed playing with our beautiful, intelligent dog, walking her, taking her for rides, and getting ice cream. She was our girl, and we loved her. One time, after playing, I ran across two rooms and flopped onto the couch. Ausia did the same—all 110 pounds landed on me. It wasn't her fault; we were playing. I immediately felt pain in my lower back. It worsened overnight, and I could barely inch my way out of bed the next morning. I foolishly did a strenuous exercise program which proved to be a bad move. My back pain was excruciating. I went to a prominent chiropractor in the area, who took care of the local sport teams, to no avail. I pursued an orthopedic surgeon, who informed me that I had a herniated disk.

I needed surgery, which went well, but I had not been advised to seek physical therapy, so I suffered another 19 years,

---

[16] Marcia Santos, https://baltimorechristianfaithcenter.com/Pastor's%20Desks/03.10.19.pdf

needlessly. The surgery alleviated the most intense pain, but not the daily pain from standing, walking, literally everything. I accepted this.

When we moved home to Erie, my new doctor mentioned physical therapy. I began immediately. Six weeks later, it was still so painful. I was going to quit but decided to go one more time. It finally clicked and gave me a new lease on life: not pain-free but so much better! What joy it was to feel like a normal person, to rise above the worst of it!

I still refuse to take pain pills and muscle-relaxants. I may need them as I age, but not now—I am only 72! I did not miss work during the 20 years I suffered and did not request help with my unknown-to-them restrictions.

Lifelong learning and education have always been important to both Tom and me. I returned to school at Carlow University, taking evening classes (after working all day) to get my bachelor's in business management. I later returned to earn my master's in professional leadership/organizational development. This was over a nine-and-a-half-year span. Tom, in the interim, earned his doctorate in administrative and policy studies. We found joy in bettering ourselves and utilizing our potential.

Who would have imagined that ten years later, I would experience the most difficult time of my life. The years flew by, and all was going well for us. I desperately wanted a baby all those years, but Tom was never *ready*. I cried, and I begged God to let me know about a baby, one way or the other. I never thought of life without a child. My soul ached. My beloved sister was blessed with seven children, and we were the aunt and uncle who spoiled and loved them. We continue to shower our love on their families, now doing so with three generations. Carol's blessings were also ours, and we will always be grateful.

Well, at age 38, Tom was finally *ready*, and a baby was on the way. It was a short, wonderful time. We bought a new house and had the room ready for our blessing. We were at the old house, having a house sale when it happened. I started to miscarry. Tom rushed me to the hospital, and I cried continuously. The kind nurse comforted me the best she could, but it was all over ... the dream of our family, crushed. The loss changed our relationship, as I was resentful that he waited so long to decide on a family. Would it have happened had I been younger? I was angry and beyond broken. We, who were so in love, best friends, and the perfect couple, grew more distant.

We separated, which was even more agonizing, and we were both devastated. We were always considered the *perfect couple*. I was scared. I felt so alone and terrified, living hours from our families in Erie. This pain was worse than death; in death, the person doesn't *choose* to leave you.

The unthinkable happened. Tom found someone else. My heart was shattered, and I was alone. What would I do now? The Lord gave me a strength like I had not known before, and I was determined to be positive and continue my journey in life.

I remember trying to hold fast to my positive attitude and spirit, so for New Year's Day, I made myself a small pork and sauerkraut dinner, desperately trying to move on. I ate and immediately went and vomited. I couldn't fool my body and mind about the toll this was taking on me: mentally, physically, and emotionally. I continued to pray, as always. I had God, so I knew I was not alone. The loss was very real, and I was in such emotional turmoil that I felt as though I were out in the middle of the ocean with no one and nothing to help me. I was lost.

Tom still loved me and felt torn. I hated him for hurting me but still loved him at the same time. God wanted us to be together. We talked and agreed to go to a weekend for married couples facing relationship difficulties, called Retrouvaille[17]. It helped us restore our marriage and taught us how to communicate on an emotional level. We worked together and built a stronger-than-ever marriage. We reconnected, and our relationship was restored. The past had passed, and we began anew.

We thank God that it worked for us. We will be married 48 years in August 2023, and it gets better with each passing day. We have such a strong, loving relationship, are best friends, and are supportive of one another. As a couple, we rescued our history together—our precious marriage—and we learned a new respect and love for one another. That was over 30 years ago. We are living our best lives now and are more appreciative than ever. God led us back together to find our truest joy in living our lives as *us*. We are of the same mindset, spiritually and emotionally, and we have intense joy that goes *beyond* happiness ... it encompasses our whole hearts and souls.

In 2001, we decided to relocate back home to Erie to care for my beloved mother. My dad had already passed, and she had difficulty getting around due to back surgery from a fall on icy stairs decades earlier. She was mostly in a wheelchair. It was my privilege, my blessing, my honor, and my joy to be there for her. I had been homesick for 27 years, and I am forever grateful for that precious time with my mom.

Around 2009, I lost my job at the age of 59 and discovered that jobs were not readily available once you get to a certain age. I thought my life was over; what would I do? I had no purpose. I felt worthless. I worked various jobs over the next few years but was still seeking joy. I prayed for guidance.

It was time to reinvent myself; I am a positive woman, after all. This time, it would be doing things I had a passion for: nurturing and mentoring others to help them live their best lives.

---

[17] Retrouvaille Marriage Help Program For Struggling Couples, https://retrouvaille.org/

I started three businesses and a Facebook page called Unwavering Women 60+: Live Your Best Life! This page reaches out to women to share articles, recipes, demos, stories, health and wellness, exercises, etc. Women helping women! What better joy exists than to help others?

I always wanted to write a book and even began one years ago; then life got in the way, and it never materialized. In 2022, I heard of an anthology and researched it. It is a collaborative book in which many authors join together, each writing a personal chapter on a specific theme. I wanted *IN* but was unable to find one. I prayed. The Lord tapped me on my shoulder and said, *Why not you?* I was terrified; how would I even begin? I held tight to my faith and put it out there. I was surprised that there was a good deal of interest, and women *did* want to share in my dream!

We hired a publisher, shared costs, and 20 women began to write their book. We were *unstoppable!* In September, we had our book launch with full media coverage and publicity. Wow, 20 women over 60! This was due to the amazing book launch committee we created and our teamwork—it was fabulous. Thus, *20 Lives Ignited: How 20 Women Over 60 are Creating Success on Their Own Terms* was born. We made the Amazon Bestseller list!

I am an aging advocate, and our message is, "You are never too old, and it is never too late to become who you want to be. Life begins at 60!" We choose our own joy.

Soon after, several women asked if I would be putting together a second anthology. I put it out there. It would be a go if at least 20 women wanted to join in. We have 22 amazing women contributing to this book, ***We Choose Joy: How 22 Women Went Beyond Healing to Create Joyful Lives!*** This book has an age span of 27 to 73 years of experience and wisdom to share. It demonstrates how 22 strong women transcended difficult times to create their own joy, and who continue to cultivate this joy. Our mission is to share this with others and to provide a roadmap as to how we did it!

"You have a choice each and every single day.
I choose to feel blessed.
I choose to feel grateful.
I choose to be excited.
I choose to be thankful.
I choose to be happy."[18]
~ Amber Housley

We seek, create, and choose our JOY ... and we've only just begun!

All glory to God!

---

[18] Amber Housley, https://www.goodreads.com/author/quotes/20526573.Amber_Housley

About Linda

Linda is a retired industrial engineer, vision board guru, multi-business owner, curator, author, creativity coach, and aging advocate. She attended evening classes for over nine years to earn up through her master's degree in professional leadership/organizational development. She is results-oriented and mentors women, providing support and direction in clarifying goals and living their best lives!

She belongs to numerous women's groups, clubs, and organizations where women support and empower one another. She strives to help people of all ages grow and live their best lives.

Curator and Author of Two Collaborative Anthologies

20 Lives Ignited: How 20 Women Over 60 are Creating Success on Their Own Terms

We Choose Joy: How 22 Women Went Beyond Healing to Create Joyful Lives

Professional Organizations

American Association of University Women (AAUW)

Coffee Club Divas (Women's Empowerment)

Professional Doll Makers Art Guild

Professional Women's Network of the Monterrey Peninsula, Ca.

The Welcome Club of Erie

The Erie Woman's Club

Education

AS Degree in Industrial Engineering Production Technology, Community College of Allegheny County

BS Degree in Business Management, Carlow University

MS Degree in Professional Leadership/Organizational Development, Carlow University

Connect with Linda:

Facebook: Linda Laird Staszewski, www.facebook.com/20livesignited

Facebook: Linda Laird Staszewski, www.facebook.com/WeChooseJOY

E-Mail: strongamazingwomen@gmail.com

JOY Is My Strength

Michelle Walker

"It is only in sorrow bad weather masters us; in joy we face the storm and defy it."[19]

~ Amelia Barr

Let's start in the beginning. In *my* beginning, *my* world was without form and void, as in the beginnings of the earth: formless and empty. That's how I felt. I grew up in an alcoholic home—literal primordial chaos. Ever since I can remember, most of what I had known was abuse at the hands of those who should have loved and protected me—physical, verbal, emotional, sexual—more than a child or adult should ever have to endure. Relatives, friends, my ex-spouse, and my parents all had a role to play.

Though my father was an alcoholic and physically and verbally abusive, I carried the weight of the trauma from my mother more than that of my father. At the age of six, my mother had a nervous breakdown. I have no recollection of what happened after she screamed at me and began beating me. I only remember my father coming home late that night and telling me and my brother that Mom was in the hospital. My mother told me what happened when I was about 25 years old. After her death in 2003, I discovered her journal. In it, she spoke of her own struggles of jealousy over me, the abuses she endured (in most cases, abuse begets abuse), and how she craved a connection with me that never came to fruition. When I read her words and how proud she

[19] Amelia Barr, https://allauthor.com/quotes/54063/

was of me, I could see the Lord beginning to heal my heart and the mother-wound it bore. I was able to grant forgiveness and receive the peace that I had longed for. I found the beginning of joy.

After walking through sexual abuse at the hands of close relatives (not my parents) and then being raped in high school, I found the attention of a man I will call "Allen," endearing. We moved in together, and I became pregnant with my first child, a daughter. He would later abandon me. However, even in that chaos, I found joy in my child, and I focused on raising her the best I could. Later, I would go on to marry my first husband, and we had two more children together. I was verbally and physically abused by him.

During this time, I went back to school to earn a medical degree. I came back from class in February of 1996 to find him gathering his things. I assumed he had to take care of something important only to find that he wasn't coming back. He sent me a "Dear Michelle" letter where he described how the thought of my success made him feel threatened. Rather than sharing that with me, he abandoned me due to his own insecurities.

As a mom of three children, I realized I couldn't provide for them and be a pre-med student. I changed my major to nursing at Georgia Southern University. This necessitated a move to Statesboro, Ga., where I met my current husband of 24 years, Michael Walker. I married him in August of 1998, following the birth of my fourth child. It was here I discovered another instance of joy. My new husband loved and cared for my first three children and was not intimidated by my possible success. I completed my bachelor of science in nursing in December of 2000, received the Spirit of Nursing Award, and was inducted as a member of Sigma Theta Tau Honor Society of Nursing. These achievements helped spark and inspire joy as my journey continued, eventually leading me to become a nurse coach and settle into a new aspect of nursing that can help bring joy to others. Little did I know, there was a storm brewing and things would change ... again.

By February 2006, my youngest child began struggling with her emotions, transitions, and defiance toward authority. In walked an oppositional defiance disorder diagnosis; however, she would receive treatment for a spectrum of mood disorders from 2009–2012. It all came to a head for us in 2012 after truancy issues and physical aggression. We placed her in an intensive therapy group home for six months. We had to admit we needed help. Letting go was the best decision we ever made. Today, she is a graduate with a bachelor's degree in geology and works in a wilderness therapy program as a support and wilderness expert for licensed professionals. She is using her skills, past experiences, and love for nature to help others. Another taste of joy.

As my youngest child struggled, a major blow struck my second daughter and my third child (my son). My two middle children are both by my ex-husband. As they returned home from a weekend visitation with him, he was acting odd. He would normally drink coffee and chat for a bit, but this time, he was in a hurry. It was strange for him. When he left, my daughter asked to talk to me and told me, "Mommy, Daddy molested me."

Chaos. Literal chaos. She would go on to testify against him and receive justice at the hands of the law. He was sentenced to serve three counts of aggravated child molestation by a jury of his peers and ten years for each charge to run concurrently. In one blow, my children lost their biological father. My daughter's innocence was sullied by the man who should've loved her the most. My son lost the main person who was to teach him what it is to be a man.

My son has since grown up to be a very kind, hard worker, who deeply cares for others. My daughter is currently in school to become a special education teacher. She is a mom of three and a good wife. All these things bring me great joy. Looking back, I learned a profound understanding of joy through each of these struggles. Life is a lot like primordial chaos. With each instance or event that happens to us, we are changed, we are shaped. The sparks and moments of joy help keep us tied to reality. They are the glimmers of hope that propel us forward when we are being beckoned to stay stuck in a dark and devoid past. Hope is a gift from God.

I never thought in a million years that I would become who I am despite my failings, let alone my children become the amazing adults they are today. If you'd have told me that my oldest would be an amazing cosmetologist, mother of three, wife, and youth minister, I'd have called you crazy. If you'd have told me that my other three would be where they are, I'd have said, *not us; not me*. This is what joy looks like. Joy is seeing outcomes that can only be from the very hand of God and experiencing moments of divine intervention where he brings good from evil. Joy is rejoicing, praise, and happiness all rolled into one beautiful emotion, even during times of great trouble. The joy God gives is my strength.

As Nehemiah 8:10 (NIV) states, "Go and enjoy choice food and sweet drinks, and send some to those who have nothing prepared. This day is holy to our Lord. Do not grieve for the joy of the Lord is your strength." The Lord has truly been my strength through this life thus far. This also brings joy. Looking back, as with the creation of the universe, it's as if God has taken the chaos, shaped it, and molded it into what it is today. As Genesis 1:31 (NIV) states, "And God saw everything that He had made, and behold, it was very good ..." This is exactly what it is: very good.

This is what joy is all about—finding the goodness growing in places where it shouldn't be possible.

About Michelle

Michelle Walker is a child of the living God and healed survivor of trauma. She attended Georgia Southern University where she earned a bachelor of science in nursing degree. In 2022, after a 21-year successful and rewarding career as the bedside nurse, Michelle studied and earned a certificate in transformative nurse coaching through the Nurse Coach Collective. She continues as a bedside nurse while coaching women and men through video and by phone, helping them to live a more authentic, expansive, and satisfying life.

Michelle and her husband, Michael, will celebrate 25 years of marriage in August of 2023. They have four children, six grandchildren, two dogs, and six chickens.

Michelle possesses a compact professional nursing license in her home state of Georgia, allowing her to coach clients as a licensed registered nurse in any state in which the compact is recognized. She is also licensed in Pennsylvania and Ohio, which at the time of writing this, are not in the multistate compact agreement.

Connect with Michelle

Email: mlynwalker@gmail.com

Facebook:
https://www.facebook.com/profile.php?id=100065145693167

Inspire! Joyfully Giving Your Unique Gifts to Life

Bonnie Zehentner

"Giving with a pure and loving heart is the force that powers the universe. Receiving with joy and gratitude is the complementary action that spins the cosmic wheel of life."

~ Bonnie Zehentner

Did you know that helping others with your personal talents is one of the most rewarding things you can do? Service to others is the key to happiness and joy in your own life. Giving with a pure heart is the secret.

When I was in grade school, my extended family got together for a large holiday party. Grandparents, aunts, uncles, and all my cousins were there. It was so much fun! We danced to the live music of my uncle's band, as laughter filled the air.

Then came time for the holiday gift exchange, with each of the cousins bringing a gift for another child. One by one, all my cousins received their gifts. I watched, anticipating what I would receive. I waited and waited ... My aunt's husband asked me if I had gotten a gift. "No," I replied. I thought, surely, he could help.

I never did get a gift that day. My parents never knew. I assumed I had been overlooked. There were so many of us, it would be easy to do. In the video, you can see me standing all alone, my long, wavy brown hair flowing onto my vibrant robin's egg blue dress, looking anxious. Yes, there was still a smile on my face.

Around this same year, my mother gave me the absolutely most valuable gift of all. She told me that I could be anything that I wanted. Imagine that? I must have taken this to heart, as you will soon see. As a teenager, I decided I would be an engineer. Unfortunately, my mother talked to a male engineer who said women weren't engineers. This put a damper on this pursuit, but I'm sure there was a mysterious reason for this. So, the fun journey began ... What do I want to be when I grow up?

First, I achieved a BFA in art with a music minor. Next, a computer programming diploma. Later, I gained a BSN in nursing. After nursing for a few years, I pursued training in several types of kinesiology, which I explain in the next paragraph. I was happy to assist others in improving their lives with techniques that went beyond conventional methods.

I used Brain Gym® peak performance designed-movements and goal-oriented balancing procedures, to assist people to move forward with life goals and do things easier. As a Health Kinesiology™ practitioner, I used gentle muscle testing to determine specifics for a balancing process that promotes better energy flow in the body, which then triggers repair from emotional and physical stress.

Then came my deep dive into classical feng shui. The key behind feng shui is that modern science says that everything is energy. According to Albert Einstein, "[M]ass and energy are both but different manifestations of the same thing [...] Furthermore, the equation E is equal to m c-squared [$E=mc^2$], in which energy is put equal to mass, multiplied by the square of the velocity of light, showed that very small amounts of mass may be converted into a very large amount of energy and vice versa."

Basically, everything is energy.

Feng shui focuses universal energy, called qi (pronounced chi), to uplift individuals, society, and the environment. Feng shui requires keen attention to detail, analysis, and mathematical calculations. So many more people could receive the benefits ... if only they knew. The environment of their home or workplace could be holding them back, or encouraging unwanted, challenging situations.

I discovered that scientifically oriented classical feng shui was so different from that in popular books. It is based on physics, astronomy, architectural design, the environment, and changing cycles of time. Sure enough, I experimented and experienced the benefits of more money, better relationships, and improved health.

Why did I pursue feng shui? Suddenly, huge relationship misunderstandings kept repeating at work... over and over again. Plus I had a long drawn-out respiratory infection that came and went, causing me to cough a lot. I chose another job that unfortunately brought similar difficulties. *There must be a cause behind this.* Could feng shui help? For some time, I was drawn to explore the fascinating deep levels of this ancient art.

We had plans to remodel the master bedroom of our new home, including removing the red carpet. In feng shui, red was never a good color for this particular bedroom, based on the year the house was built and the precise compass direction. It was also the worst color for the changing yearly energy cycle, which compounded the problem. The red was removed.

I placed décor made out of one specific feng shui element in the bedroom as a remedy. The five elements are wood, fire colors, earth, metal, and water, which change the energy of the environment. Thank goodness my health and relationships improved!

My husband and I were providing 24/7 care for my father when we moved to a new home. I was also an RN. For over four years, I desired to add a few more nursing hours at a work situation that I really enjoyed. I applied feng shui technology, by placing a large water fountain outside my house in a specific direction to intentionally produce more money.

It really worked! My potential to bring in money increased so much that I had a choice to work up to 55 hours weekly. I happily accepted what fit into my busy schedule. Wow! This was certainly much more than I ever expected. Yay for the power of feng shui!

There is a universal law of giving and receiving. *When we give, we receive. When we receive, we give.* If people receive things that they have not worked for or earned, they often mentally assign less value to them. Sometimes appreciation and value are directly related to the personal effort and money one has invested. This increases the perceived benefit.

Giving without expecting anything in return is a heart-felt enhancement to life. Yet, if you are in business, you must first receive to be able to give and be a philanthropist. A gift from the receiver acknowledges that they value you and your talents. It is the natural flow of the universe.

The Key!

"Receiving is fantastic ... yet the real key to *awesome success is giving from the heart*. Loving service is your cosmic gift to life."

Feng shui remedies enhance good qualities, boost success, and minimize potentially challenging aspects. However, the key is to put these remedies into action. Did the person place remedies or are they expecting fairytale results ... like waving a magic wand?

This magical thinking analogy works in all areas of life. Do you have goals? Are you willing to write them down on paper? Are you taking action to achieve your dreams? Or do you simply sit back and wonder where all the time has gone?

Did you know that gratitude assists people to manifest their goals? It is true. Expressing more gratitude could also make you happier, healthier, and more successful.

When you start looking for things, people, and events to be grateful for, it tells the subconscious mind to be on the lookout ... that gratitude is valuable. You will start noticing more positive attributes in people and things.

When you express more gratitude, you may be very surprised how many things you have to be grateful for!

Goal Setting Keys

What are the key components to effective goal setting? What are your dreams? What would you like? First, the goal topic must be something positive. Use positive words. Avoid words like "no," "not," "should," or "could." Say it in the present tense, which is in the now. "I" or "my" statements work well for this.

Setting a timeline to achieve your goal could make it easier to manifest your dream. It could be weeks, months, or even a year or more for a really big goal. If you are still working on the goal at the specified time, simply set a new date. Flexibility is a key to greater success.

The goal must grab your interest, desire, and enthusiasm. Did you know that challenging goals are more likely to be accomplished? A goal is something that you would like. Something that is action packed and energizes you to reach beyond your current status.

Finally, set clear intentions so you can achieve the desired outcome. *Charge up your life with powerful goals!*

7 Goal Tips

1. Formulate a positive goal stated in the present time.
2. Write the goal down on paper.
3. Write steps, especially for large goals.
4. Take consistent action.
5. Keep a success and gratitude journal.
6. Believe in yourself. Keep taking action. Be flexible.
7. Celebrate the success of manifesting your goal!

My most recent accomplishment is writing. I never liked English class in school. Math was definitely a favorite. Who would have ever guessed? Yet, I have written two books... here I sit typing away, writing this for you. I am also excited to share that my first book, on classical feng shui, includes many holistic and personal success tips.

Your key to a happier life is to take action toward achieving your goals. I am grateful for having had so much fun on my life's journey of discovering many ways to assist others.

I challenge you to be brave. Have courage to do some of the things that you really love. Overcome inertia and potential fear of moving forward, by courageously pursuing your dreams. Believe in yourself to achieve! Enjoy the exquisite vitality you experience when sharing your very own unique gifts and talents.

My journey of discovery has taken me on such a wonderful adventure. Who would have ever known that the little girl in the blue dress would have so many uplifting experiences and turns in the road as she searched for her life's calling?

The mysterious guiding hand knew exactly what that little girl needed to expand and grow. It has led her way beyond her aspiration to be an engineer... to share unconventional holistic methods that assist others to create greater happiness and success in life. I overcame many challenges by using keys from my very own treasure box. The most surprising benefit was from feng shui.

Today, I truly embrace the joy of being *a vibrant holistic lady*. May you *easily* find your own successful way to express your unique gifts and blessings. I hope that you enjoy your journey of sharing your special gifts and treasures with life as much as I do.

The journey lasts a lifetime...

About Bonnie

Bonnie Zehentner, BFA, BSN, RN

Bonnie loves assisting people to achieve greater harmony and energized vitality, as well as increased happiness, better relationships, and improved success in life!

Bonnie is a Classical-Feng shui master consultant, Licensed Brain Gym® instructor, and Health Kinesiology™ practitioner. Her diverse background includes display artist, various business positions, and director of nursing.

Books

- *168 FENG SHUI Tips for the Home Office and More: Plus Holistic and Personal Success Keys*
- *Upcoming book in 2023, which contains 168 holistic keys to boost your happiness and success*

To learn how to create greater joy, vitality, and prosperity in your own life, you may—

Connect with Bonnie

www.harmonic-zone.com (Online services offered)

Email: harmoniczone@yahoo.com

Printed in the USA
CPSIA information can be obtained
at www.ICGtesting.com
LVHW022031101223
766158LV00005B/287